Annie Bell

gorgeouschristmas

Annie Bell

gorgeouschristmas

Over 100 Delicious Fail-Safe Recipes to Fill Your Holiday with Joy

with photographs by Chris Alack

Kyle Books

This edition published in 2010 by Kyle Books
An imprint of Kyle Cathie Limited
www.kylecathie.com

Distributed by National Book Network
4501 Forbes Blvd., Suite 200
Lanham, MD 20706
Phone: (800) 462 6420

First published in Great Britain in 2009 by Kyle Cathie Limited

ISBN 978-1-906868-07-9

The Library of Congress Cataloging-in-Publication Data is available on file.

10 9 8 7 6 5 4 3 2 1

Editor: Suzanna de Jong
Design: pinkstripedesign@hotmail.com
Copy Editor: Annie Lee
Proofreader: Kay Halsey
Indexer: Alex Corrin
Americanizer: Elizabeth Brais
Photographer: Chris Alack
Home Economist: Kim Morphew
Prop Stylist: Sue Radcliffe
Production: Lisa Pinnell

Color reproduction: SC (Sang Choy) International Pte Ltd, Singapore
Printed and bound in Singapore by Star Standard Industries Pty Ltd

contents

introduction

Christmas is a time of pure magic. For those of us who take it seriously it is a season within a season, one we anticipate for weeks and sometimes months in advance. Where will we be, what will we be doing, who will we be celebrating with, and of course what will we be eating? The day itself, though, is only part of the season, and the run-up is just as much if not more fun, with all that planning and dreaming. The shopping, parties, and celebrating hit a high note from the end of November. Even if we say we're not going to do anything about Christmas until December, for most of us this is a rule that lasts about as long as our New Year's resolution.

Visual charm is writ large in the cooking we aspire to at Christmas. I have a horror of "tasteful" or "designer" Christmases: trees, cards, cakes, you name it. Bring on the glitter and colored lights, the kitsch Christmas tree decorations, the ceramic Santa or nativity scene that kept you enraptured as a child, those rusting cookie cutters and vintage cake decorations. One of the joys of being that little bit older is that Christmas had yet to be invaded by commercial merchandizing. I would rather travel back to an age of innocence, even if it does mean making paper chains on my own.

So retro it is. Our love of Christmas has everything to do with our childhood, trying to recreate what we left behind. And as soon as we have children that urge becomes compulsive. So pity those couples who grew up with very different traditions, trying to agree on what the order of the day should be. In our house, thankfully, that goes little further than, "Should we have Christmas lunch [my way] or Christmas dinner [his way]."

The good news is how readily the food brings those memories flooding back. It doesn't have to be wildly ambitious, technically brilliant, or even the finest money can buy. If your mom always served pigs in a blanket with the drinks before the roast, that's what will do it for you. Memory underwrites our sense of smell, so whenever we taste and draw in all those lovely Christmas scents, we travel back to happy childhood times. None of the recipes here seek to rewrite history. They are mainly based on my own traditional English childhood

Christmases, with an eye to exploiting some more alluring modern trends like sherry and quince-glazed ham and bûche de Noël.

Christmas Eve was a time of hushed anticipation in our house, with children parked in front of a movie while my mother tried to get ahead with the preparation for Christmas lunch and make sure the house was ready. The party proper would begin that evening. And then Christmas morning arrived, with glittery felt stockings groaning with treasure laid at the end of the bed. We all traipsed off to church, everyone in their Christmas best, then home for Champagne, presents under the tree, and a huge traditional lunch. This was played out year after year, the same pattern and the same food, most of which I now cook for my own family.

And I love revisiting these traditions: how can you be bored with that roast turkey and Christmas pudding when they only come around once a year? So the chapters that follow seek to cover all my favorites, and to cater for all the different occasions. Kicking off is Finger Foods, nothing as complex as a canapé, but relaxed and yummy eats like miniature sausage rolls, smoked salmon blinis, toasted Stilton and pickled walnut sandwiches, and devils on horseback. Little Pots & Big Pies covers small savories and pâtés for eating with toast and a bowl of soup, and hearty meaty pies you can make well in advance, great for a hungry horde.

Gorgeous Birds and All the Trimmings do what they say, and hopefully you will find every possible side dish you could wish for, a special way with bread sauce, cranberry sauce, honey-mustard roast chipolatas, and lots of stuffings. And it doesn't have to be the traditional English turkey—roast goose, roast duck,

or partridge with crispy crumbs and bacon sing just as loudly. Finally there are all those lovely soups and toasted sandwiches that follow with the leftovers.

On to the sweet chapters: Christmas is a time when you can go to town with lovely baked goodies and desserts, and chocolates to make and give. The Christmas pudding recipe was handed down to me by my grandmother, and is a vintage classic, while white Christmas cheesecake is a new addition to the repertoire, as is the traditional French Twelfth Night cake, something to celebrate with around New Year.

Honestly, I do sometimes muse on an easy Christmas, and in that sense know I am my own worst enemy. It is the cook who sets the guidelines: whether to make stuffing or accept the butcher's offer to stuff the bird for you, whether to exploit the local pâtisserie and order a bûche de Noël or to make it at home. The last thing I want anyone to feel is that they have to prepare absolutely everything from scratch. I hope I have covered everything you might want to make, but that doesn't mean you should be trying to make it all.

My family always tease me about my lists: I have lists for everything, and they grow in number and length the closer we get to Christmas. But it's advance planning that ensures you actually enjoy the festivities yourself. Any cooking you do in the days leading to the run-up will be time well invested. With carefully planned menus you'll spend minimum time in the kitchen during the days after Christmas, and gear up again for New Year's Eve. That said, the more helping hands the better; if the work's shared it won't seem like a burden. There are plenty of jobs that don't require any skill, like peeling potatoes, grating cheese, or making a stock.

I try to balance things, and the easy route comes in the form of luxury. I intersperse things I've made myself with simple dishes of smoked salmon or eel, oysters, and king shrimp with mayonnaise, watercress, and fine bread. Or a selection of lovely cheeses warmed beside the fire for a couple of hours, with prosciutto, chicory leaves, and walnuts. Parfaits and pâtés too will see you through meals and cocktail nibbles, spread on to blinis or toast, while desserts can take advantage of all those fruits in brandy, such as cherries, spooned over ice cream, or can just be a couple of chocolate truffles. Think of Christmas dinner itself as a very big Sunday lunch, and it doesn't feel so daunting. All that's left is to enjoy it all. *Santé*.

the art of decoration

Part of the fun of making Christmas cakes and desserts lies with decorating them. I tend to start collecting candy canes, marshmallow snowmen, and gold dragees while I'm out Christmas shopping. But there are plenty of on-line shops that help. Try Amazon (www.amazon.com); The Baker's Nook (www.ShopBakersNook.com); Country Kitchen Sweetart (www.countrykitchenusa.com); Millcreek Country Store (www.MillcreekCountryStore.com); Pattycakes (www.shop.pattycakes.com); and Sugarcraft (www.sugarcraft.com).

bowls & racks

I always make my Christmas puddings in Mason Cash pudding basins, and mix them in an old-fashioned cane-weave mixing bowl (www.pacificmerchants.com).

When roasting a goose or duck, a rack will ensure that the fat runs off into the base of the roasting dish, allowing the bird to crisp and color all over. Le Creuset (www.lecreuset.co.uk) produce two special racks that fit within their roasting dishes, with handles for ease of lifting the bird out at the end.

finger foods

The exhilarating pop of a Champagne cork and gentle hiss of foam brings with it the most vexing of the season's demands, cocktail nibbles. Thinking in miniature is the last thing we have time to do in between all that wrapping and last-minute shopping. To which there is one immediate solution. Banish all thoughts of anything complicated that will go down in one bite, and plan for finger foods that are a little bit bigger.

Things on toast, small sausage rolls, and generous mouthfuls of smoked salmon are altogether more relaxing and homely than miniature quiches and doll's house canapés. Their role, after all, is to take the edge off our hunger before dinner, but equally, if you keep them coming, followed by dessert towards the end, they will also replace dinner. So it can be a lovely way of entertaining lots of friends and family without all the work that goes into preparing a large meal.

In England, old-fashioned savories get wolfed down and make hearty no-nonsense appetizers. They are spiced with distinctly British notes like mace and Worcestershire sauce, mustard, and capers. The most famous are rarebits, angels and devils on horseback, and anchovies with scrambled eggs, known as a Scotch woodcock. Deviled chicken livers and kidneys are also popular, and I have a soft spot for herring roe on toast.

The buttery scent of pastry emerging from the oven as you walk through the door makes the best possible welcome. I marvel at puff pastry and the way it rises within minutes to exquisite gossamer-fine layers. Crisp straws and little biscuits make a star turn at any cocktail party, and their delicacy and prettiness belie the speed and ease of preparation. To their credit, such pastries can also be prepared several days in advance and reheated for a few minutes before serving.

Few can resist a homemade cheese straw—I certainly can't. The best ones taste like that crispy bit of toasted cheese on the bottom of the frying pan after you've cooked a grilled cheese. I find a mixture of Gruyère and Parmesan gives a good balance of flavor and crunch.

cheese straws

8 ounces puff pastry
2½ tablespoons freshly grated
   Parmesan
3½ tablespoons grated Gruyère
a knife tip of cayenne pepper
1 egg yolk, blended with
   1 tablespoon milk
peanut or vegetable oil

Serves 8
Makes 20–25

Preheat the oven to 400°F. Thinly roll out the pastry on a lightly floured surface into a large rectangle about 12 x 20 inches wide. Place the long sides facing you, and trim them. Combine the Parmesan and Gruyère with the cayenne pepper in a bowl and scatter on top of half of the pastry, leaving a ½-inch edge. Brush this with the egg wash and bring the lower edge up over it. Roll the sheet to seal the edges and compress the cheese—you should have a strip about 6 inches wide. Cut this into ½-inch straws.

Holding one end in either hand, twist each strip to give you about 5 turns, and lay them ¾ inch apart on one or two oiled baking sheets, pressing the edges down well to ensure they don't unravel as they cook. Bake for 12–15 minutes, until they are evenly golden, turning the trays around halfway through. The bottom tray may take a few minutes longer than the top.

Loosen the straws with an offset spatula (any that break are the cook's tip), and ideally serve while still warm, or newly cooled. I like to stack them in glasses, but alternatively you can arrange them in a bowl or on a plate. They can also be stored for several days in an airtight container, and reheated for 5 minutes in an oven preheated to 300°F.

We are so used to the convenience of ready-roasted nuts that we have all but forgotten what a treat they are freshly roasted and salted, when they have that wonderful squeaky-clean bite. You also get to combine all your favorites for a tailor-made mix. I have a particular fondness for roasted almonds, cashews, and macadamias, with dried cherries for festive cheer.

christmas fruit and nuts

2 teaspoons unsalted butter, softened

1 cup cashews

1 cup almonds, peeled

1 cup macadamias

3 tablespoons coarse sea salt

cayenne pepper

½ cup dried cherries or cranberries

Serves 8

Preheat the oven to 300°F. Grease a cookie sheet with the butter and spread the cashews and almonds in a single layer on top. Bake for 10 minutes, then scatter the macadamias on top. Bake for another 35 minutes, by which time they should be a pale creamy gold.

Scatter the sea salt over a sheet of parchment paper. Spread the nuts on top and use a teaspoon to toss and rub the salt through them. Wrap the paper up into a package and set aside overnight (the minimum they need is 1 hour if you are doing them at the last minute). On unwrapping the nuts, dust them with a generous knife tip of cayenne pepper and shake off the excess salt. Transfer to a bowl and mix in the dried cherries or cranberries.

This three-in-one looks as though you've gone to a great deal of trouble, when in truth it's just one recipe, with the dough flavored in three different ways. They're deliciously short and buttery, and way, way better than anything you are likely to be able to buy.

cocktail shortbreads

Dough

1½ cups all-purpose flour

1 cup ground almonds

11 tablespoons salted butter, chilled
   and diced

Flavorings

1 heaping teaspoon poppy seeds,
   plus extra for rolling

finely grated zest of 1 lemon

1 heaping teaspoon sesame seeds,
   plus extra for rolling

½ teaspoon ground cumin

2½ tablespoons freshly grated
   Parmesan

cayenne pepper

vegetable oil

Serves 10

Place the flour, ground almonds, and butter in the bowl of a food processor and briefly process to fine crumbs—it's important to heed the "briefly" here.

Divide the mixture between three bowls. Stir the poppy seeds and lemon zest into one, the sesame seeds and cumin into the other, and the Parmesan and a hint of cayenne pepper into the third bowl. Bring each mixture together into a ball, using your hands. Form the cheese dough into a roughly shaped sausage about 1 inch in diameter, wrap it in plastic wrap and give it a roll to smooth it out. Wrap the remaining two balls of dough in plastic wrap. You can freeze them at this point, otherwise chill them all for an hour or two.

Preheat the oven to 300°F, and brush a couple of cookie sheets with oil. Knead the poppy seed dough until it is pliable, then roll pieces into balls a little smaller than a cherry, roll them in poppy seeds in a small bowl, and place slightly apart on a baking sheet. Repeat this with the sesame seed dough, this time rolling them into a slightly elongated shape and coating them in sesame seeds, then slice the roll of cheese dough about ½ inch thick. Bake the biscuits for 35–40 minutes, until the cheese ones are lightly golden, by which time the others will also be cooked inside. Loosen the cheese biscuits with an offset spatula, and leave them all to cool. They will keep well for up to a week in an airtight container.

Like cocktail sausages, a plate of these handed round comes back empty within minutes. Delicious served warm from the oven, you can also make them in advance. If you can find puff pastry made with butter, so much the better. And as ever, your best bet with sausage meat is a sausage with a good pedigree—simply slip off the skin.

miniature sausage rolls

9 ounces puff pastry

½ pound sausage meat

1 teaspoon Dijon mustard

1 teaspoon wholegrain mustard

1 egg yolk, whisked with

   1 tablespoon milk

Serves 6

Preheat the oven to 400°F. Thinly roll out the pastry on a lightly floured surface into a rectangle the width of a sheet of 8½ x 11 paper. Trim the long edges and cut this into two finger-long strips, about 3 inches wide. Using your hands, divide the sausage meat between the strips, rolling it into a long thin cylinder a little fatter than your finger, and laying it down the length of the pastry. Blend the mustards together and use a knife to smear this mixture in a line down the length of sausage meat.

Paint one long edge of each piece of pastry with a ½-inch rim of egg wash. Fold the unpainted edge over the sausage meat, and then the painted edge on top and press together. Trim the ends of excess pastry, and if necessary cut the sausage rolls in half to fit a cookie sheet, sealed side down. Score the top of the sausage rolls with diagonal slits ½ inch apart, and paint the top and sides with egg wash. Bake for 25–30 minutes.

Leave to cool for 15 minutes, then cut diagonally into 1-inch slices and serve warm as an appetizer. They can also be rewarmed for 10 minutes in an oven preheated to 300°F.

These elegant little cocktail biscuits have for so long featured at all the best cocktail parties. I find it easiest to roll out a sheet of puff pastry, rather than a piece from a block. You can make up the roll and keep it in the fridge for several days, ready to slice and bake.

catherine wheels

approx. 7 saffron filaments
6 salted anchovy fillets, finely chopped
3 tablespoons unsalted butter,
  softened
approx. 8 ounces puff pastry,

Serves 6–8
Makes approx. 25

Grind the saffron filaments in a pestle and mortar, then add the chopped anchovies, and work to a paste. Add the butter and blend.

Assuming you are using a sheet of pastry, roll this into a rectangle about 8–10 x 12 inches on a lightly floured work surface and trim the short sides. Spread the butter over the surface and roll the pastry back up again into a long thin tube about ¾ inch in diameter, starting with a short side. Wrap in plastic wrap and chill for a couple of hours or overnight.

Preheat the oven to 350°F. Carefully slice the roll into rounds just under a ½ inch thick, ideally using a small serrated knife to avoid squashing them, discarding the ends. Lay these on a cookie sheet spaced slightly apart, weigh them down with another cookie sheet, and bake for 12–15 minutes. Serve warm or at room temperature. They can also be rewarmed for 5 minutes in an oven preheated to 350°F.

Little toasted sandwiches are exactly what you feel like with that second glass of Champagne, when dinner still seems a way off. These are just enough to warm you and take the edge off your hunger without ruining your appetite altogether. The sweetness of pickled walnuts makes them an ideal relish for Stilton.

toasted stilton and pickled walnut sandwiches

unsalted butter, softened

4 slices of whole-wheat or other nutty
    brown bread

3 ounces Stilton (weight excluding
    rind), sliced

3 pickled walnuts, sliced

a few slivers of red onion

sprigs of watercress to garnish

Serves 4

Butter the bread on both sides. Cover two of the slices with a layer of Stilton, then add the pickled walnuts and onion. Close the sandwiches with the top layer of bread and press down. They can be prepared to this point in advance.

If you have a sandwich toaster, you can cook them in this. Otherwise, heat a large frying pan (ideally non-stick) over high heat for several minutes, or two pans if one can't hold both sandwiches at once. Place the sandwiches in the pan, turn the heat down to medium low and cook for 3–5 minutes on each side, until golden on the outside and oozing melted cheese. Using a sharp knife, cut the crusts off the toasted sandwiches and slice each one into four triangles. Serve with a few sprigs of watercress.

These need no introduction: crisp rolls of bacon encasing a jammy prune soaked in tea and port. I find I get more evenly gold and crisp devils by roasting them in a hot oven rather than fussing over a frying pan.

devils on horseback

12 pitted prunes
2 tablespoons port
4 tablespoons tea
12 slices bacon
1 tablespoon honey mustard

Serves 4–6
Makes 12

Submerge the prunes in the port and tea in a small bowl, and leave to soak overnight.

Preheat the oven to 475°F. Drain off any residual liquid from the prunes, and lay the bacon slices on a board. Brush a little mustard down the length of each slice and roll it around a prune. Place the rolls spaced slightly apart in a roasting dish, and roast for 12 minutes until golden and crisp, turning them halfway through and using an offset spatula to loosen them. Leave standing for 5–10 minutes, then skewer a cocktail stick through the bacon and serve.

I didn't try herring roe until I was well into my twenties, in a West Country pub having supper with my father. It was dished up on buttered, crisp brown toast with a squeeze of lemon and lots of chopped parsley, and I've been a fan ever since. An affordable delicacy, it's hugely underrated.

herring roe on toast

3½ tablespoons unsalted butter, plus
   extra for the toast
½ pound herring roe
½ cup all-purpose flour, seasoned
   with sea salt and black pepper
4 slices unsweetened brioche or
   white bread
1 tablespoon capers, rinsed
1 tablespoon chopped, fresh,
   flat-leaf parsley
4 lemon wedges to serve

Serves 4

Melt the butter in a small saucepan over gentle heat, skim off the surface foam, decant the clear liquid, and discard the milky residue at the bottom. You will need to fry the roe in two batches. Heat half the clarified butter in a large frying pan over medium-high heat, dust the roe in the seasoned flour, and cook for 1–2 minutes each side, until lightly colored. Move to a plate and cook the remainder in the same fashion.

While cooking the roe, toast and butter the brioche or bread. Cut the crusts off each slice and halve into slices. Divide the roe between them, scatter the capers and parsley on top, and serve with the lemon wedges.

I suppose anything threaded on to a cocktail stick might be seen as complex, but these do lie at the utilitarian end of dainty, and slip down very well. As light as a morsel of sushi, and so good with Champagne.

smoked salmon and shrimp skewers

5½ ounces smoked salmon, cut into broad strips, approx. 8 x 1½ inches
approx. 18 cooked and peeled jumbo shrimp (3–3½ ounces)
a squeeze of lemon juice
black pepper
finely chopped fresh chives or flat-leaf parsley

Serves 6–8
Makes approx. 18

Roll up each strip of smoked salmon and skewer it with a cocktail stick, then pop a shrimp on to the end curved side first. Arrange these on a plate. Cover and chill until required. To serve, squeeze a little lemon juice, grind some black pepper, and scatter chives or parsley on top.

These are my great standby for impromptu cocktail parties; they're so easy and they always go down well. To which end I make sure I always have a packet or two of blinis, some smoked salmon, and keta roe in the fridge over Christmas.

You could also serve the smoked salmon on small plates with a fork to eat standing around. In this case double the amount of smoked salmon, halve each slice into two long strips about 2 inches wide, and arrange on one or two plates. Just before eating squeeze a little lemon juice over the salmon and season with black pepper. Accompany with the keta roe and warm blinis for everyone to help themselves.

blinis with smoked salmon

¾ cup Greek yogurt

3½ ounce jar of salmon keta roe

6 ounces sliced smoked salmon, brown meat cut out

approx. 24 cocktail blinis

½ lemon

black pepper

Serves 6–8
Makes approx. 24

Spoon the Greek yogurt into a bowl and gently fold in the keta roe. Transfer to a small clean bowl. Cut the smoked salmon into approx. 2-inch morsels. If making these in advance, cover the keta roe and salmon with plastic wrap and reserve in a cool place or chill. Bring to room temperature 30 minutes before serving.

To serve, preheat the oven to 350°F. Lay the blinis out on one or two baking sheets and warm through for 2–3 minutes. Spoon ½ teaspoon or so of the keta roe on to each blini, add a folded piece of salmon, squeeze a little lemon over each, and grind some black pepper on top.

party drinks

mulled rosé

1 bottle of rosé
½ cup Cointreau
3 star anise
10 cloves
3 thin slices of clementine or satsuma
1 x 3-inch cinnamon stick
2 tablespoons fresh inner rose petals or 1 tablespoon dried rosebuds

Serves 6

Place all the ingredients except for the rose petals or buds in a small saucepan and gently heat, without allowing the wine to boil. Leave to infuse for a few minutes, then scatter the rose petals or buds on top and ladle into small cups or glasses, first popping in a metal teaspoon to stop them cracking. You could also transfer the mulled wine to a glass bowl to serve, but again protect it first with a metal spoon.

kir normand

2 tablespoons crème de cassis
1 bottle of sparkling cider, chilled

Serves 6

Spoon a teaspoon of cassis into six wine glasses and top up with very cold sparkling cider.

seville cocktails

1 cup sweet sherry (e.g. Harveys Bristol Cream)
¼ cup vodka
½ cup fresh orange juice
ice cubes
slivers of orange and a few coffee beans

Serves 6

Stir the sherry, vodka, and orange juice in a pitcher with ice, some slivers of orange, and a few coffee beans. Stir and serve.

ginger nectar

1 cup ginger wine
¾–1 cup amaretto
2 tablespoons brandy
1 cup still mineral water
2 knobs of ginger in syrup, thinly sliced
3 thin slices of lemon, halved into half moons
ice cubes

Serves 6

You can chill the bottles before mixing the cocktails, but it's not essential. Combine the ginger wine, amaretto, brandy, and mineral water in a pitcher and stir to blend, then add the sliced ginger and lemon. Add lots of ice cubes, stir, and serve.

cranberry bellinis

2 cups cranberries
⅓ cup superfine sugar
⅔ cup fresh orange juice
1 bottle of chilled Champagne or prosecco

Serves 6

Place the cranberries, sugar, and orange juice in
a small saucepan and bring to a boil. Cover the
pan and simmer over a low heat for 5 minutes
until soft, then press through a fine-mesh sieve
and leave to cool. You should have about ¾–1 cup
of thin purée. Cover and chill.

Give the purée a stir, then spoon a rounded
tablespoon into six glasses, fill up with bubbly,
and give it a quick twirl to blend.

little pots
and big pies

Little potted savories and big hearty pies have endless appeal. It must have something to do with how they are served—food that is neatly contained is particularly comforting. And all these dishes can be made in advance, so they perfectly balance out Christmas dinner, which with all the planning in the world is a last-minute juggling act, best performed on one too few glasses of Champagne. Whereas here you can separate out the work from the event.

The chicken liver parfait is a classic, and as close as you can get to foie gras without guilt. Its main sin is the amount of butter, which accounts for its luxurious melt-in-the-mouth feel. Along with the spicy smoked salmon, this is another of my last-minute cocktails stand-bys, spread on little pieces of toast with a smidgen of chutney. And with all those soups to come once you've finished up the roast, it completes supper, with generous slabs of toasted sourdough or whole wheat bread and a pile of plump, peppery watercress. But for those who want to go the extra mile for a "proper" pâté, the duck and pistachio terrine is a little bit more formal, but without demanding that you make best friends with the butcher in advance to acquire the necessary elusive cuts of meat that are a terrine-maker's staple.

Beef pies are always a hit with family and friends, but the real favorite in our house is a retro turkey and ham number, a good old-fashioned potato-topped pie that makes the most of all the leftovers. And Christmas and New Year's Eve are the perfect times to be eating a fish pie, as you're bound to be hitting the shops in the day or so beforehand, so you can relish eating it really fresh and then settle to more meaty fare in the days to come. This boulangère pie rings the changes with a top of finely sliced potatoes, in lieu of mashed, that turn deliciously crispy at the edges.

Glamorous jarred savories that can be made in a jiffy are endlessly useful. One advantage of making your own is being able to pack them into a pretty dish or little jars. They make great presents, especially if you're going to a friend's for dinner. While if you're at home, you have instant party food piled on to blinis with drinks, or a light supper with thin crisp toast and a little salad. Some lightly cooked quail's eggs or a poached egg would be delicious with the buttery salmon too.

spicy smoked salmon

14 tablespoons unsalted butter

1¼ pound smoked salmon, skinned and flaked

Tabasco

2 tablespoons small capers, plus a few extra to decorate

2 teaspoons finely chopped fresh tarragon, plus a few sprigs or leaves to decorate

1 tablespoon finely chopped fresh flat-leaf parsley

juice of ½ lemon

Serves 6

Melt half the butter in a large frying pan, add the fish, and stir to coat. Season with a few splashes of Tabasco, and stir in the capers, herbs, and lemon juice. Press the mixture into a bowl, about 1 quart in volume, or into small ramekins. Cover with plastic wrap and chill for an hour until it has begun to set.

Drape a few sprigs or leaves of tarragon over the surface, scatter a few more capers on top, then melt the remaining butter and pour this on top, submerging the herbs. Cover the dish and chill for several hours or overnight.

If you have to choose just one pâté to have on hand over Christmas, this supremely simple buttery parfait will see you through. And as with other pâtés, a green salad, some toasted sourdough, and a jar of chutney alongside and you have dinner fit for a king.

chicken liver parfait

½ pound unsalted butter

½ pound chicken livers, fatty
   membranes removed

1 bay leaf

2 sprigs of fresh thyme

sea salt, black pepper

1 shallot, peeled and finely chopped

1 garlic clove, peeled and
   finely chopped

2 tablespoons sweet wine or sherry

2 tablespoons Armagnac or brandy

1 tablespoon sour cream

freshly grated nutmeg

½–¾ ounce summer truffles,
   finely chopped (optional)

bay leaves and green or pink
   peppercorns to decorate

Serves 6

Melt 2 tablespoons of the butter in a large frying pan over medium heat. When the foam starts to subside, add the chicken livers and the herbs, season, and cook for 3 minutes, until they are golden on the outside but still pink in the center, turning the livers halfway through. Discard the herbs and put the livers with any juices into a blender.

Add another dollop of butter to the pan and cook the shallot and garlic gently for a couple of minutes until glossy and translucent. Add the sweet wine or sherry and the brandy and simmer until the liquid has all but disappeared. Put the contents of the frying pan into the blender, add the sour cream, and purée. Leave to cool for about 20 minutes.

Dice the remaining butter, add to the blender, and blend until the parfait is really smooth and creamy. Add a pinch of nutmeg and adjust the seasoning. I like to pass the parfait through a fine sieve to ensure it's as silky as possible, but you don't have to. Stir in the truffle if including. Spoon the pâté into a bowl, smooth the surface, and decorate with bay leaves and peppercorns. Cover and either freeze or chill. It keeps well for several days in the fridge. Take it out of the fridge 20 minutes before serving to soften it.

This derives from our local gastropub in London, the Havelock, where they make a mean terrine. Don't be put off by all the draining—it's important to extract the liquid so that the terrine holds together. This is good dished up with a leafy salad.

duck and pistachio terrine

4–6 slices of air-dried ham,
 e.g. prosciutto
6–8 duck breasts (approx. 3 pounds)
1¼ cups sour cream
3 medium egg yolks
sea salt
1 tablespoon green peppercorns,
 rinsed and finely chopped
1 tablespoon fresh tarragon leaves
¼–½ cup roasted pistachios, peeled
chutney and toasted sourdough
 to serve

Serves 6

Heat the oven to 275°F. Arrange the slices of ham widthwise in a 9-inch loaf pan so they overlap, draping the ends up the sides. Placing the duck breasts fat side down on the chopping board, finely slice across the breast to give three or four fine escalopes, reserving the fat if wished*.

Whisk the sour cream and egg yolks in a large bowl, season with salt, and stir in the peppercorns. Add the duck slices about a third at a time to the bowl, lightly seasoning them with salt first, and toss to coat with the mixture. Lay the duck slices in the terrine, scattering the tarragon leaves and pistachios on top as you go. Fold any overhanging ham over the top, then cover the terrine with foil. Place the pan in a roasting dish, with boiling water to come three-quarters of the way up the sides, and bake for 1 hour. Drain off the juices that have collected around the terrine, leave it to cool covered with foil, and then drain it again. Cut out a piece of cardboard to fit the top, weight it with a couple of cans or jars and chill overnight.

If any more liquid has collected, drain this off, run a knife around the terrine, and turn it over on to a plate or board. Using paper towel, gently wipe the surface of the ham to tidy it up. Cut into thick slices using a sharp knife, and accompany with chutney and toasted sourdough.

*With all those potatoes to roast over Christmas you can make good use of the duck fat. Slice and gently heat it in an oven preheated to 275°F for 30 minutes. Strain the rendered fat into a bowl, cool, then cover and chill.

No one is expecting you to mix up little soufflés as the gateway to dinner or to alleviate a light appetite, so how timely to be able to whip them out of the freezer straight into the oven for a little instant luxury. A great one for any lone vegetarians present who might otherwise miss out with all the meaty fare on offer.

mushroom soufflés

Molds

5 tablespoons unsalted butter
3 tablespoons freshly grated Parmesan

Soufflé

3⅓ cups chestnut or wild mushrooms,
    picked over and trimmed
4 tablespoons unsalted butter
sea salt, black pepper
⅓ cup all-purpose flour
approx. 1 cup whole milk
3 tablespoons freshly grated Parmesan
freshly grated nutmeg
3 medium egg yolks
5 medium egg whites

Serves 6

To prepare the molds, clarify the butter by melting it in a small saucepan. Skim off the white foam on the surface and pour off the clear yellow liquid, leaving behind the milky residue in the base. Coat the inside of six 4-ounce ramekins with the clarified butter and dust them with the Parmesan. Chill the dishes until the coating firms.

To make the soufflé, finely chop the mushrooms in a food processor. Melt half the butter in a large frying pan over medium heat, add the mushrooms, season, and fry for 6–9 minutes, until the mixture appears dry and the pieces of mushroom are separating. Melt the remaining butter in a small non-stick saucepan, stir in the flour, and cook the roux for a couple of minutes. Take off the heat and very gradually incorporate the milk, then bring the sauce to a boil and simmer over low heat for 4 minutes, stirring frequently. Remove the pan from the heat, stir in 2 tablespoons of Parmesan and the mushrooms, and season with salt, pepper, and nutmeg. Allow to cool for a few minutes, then beat in the egg yolks and transfer to a large bowl.

Preheat the oven to 375°F. Whisk the egg whites in another large bowl until stiff. Fold a couple of spoons of the whisked egg white into the sauce to lighten it and then fold in the remainder in two batches. Pour the soufflé mixture into the dishes and scatter the rest of the Parmesan evenly over the surface. The soufflés can be frozen at this point, in which case cover and put them into the freezer without delay. Otherwise place them on a cookie sheet, place it immediately in the oven, and cook for about 9–11 minutes. Avoid opening the door; the soufflés should ideally be slightly moist in the center. If cooking them from frozen allow 17–20 minutes.

These miniature pies offer up the best bits of steak and kidney and cottage pie rolled into one, nuggets of meat and lots of lovely rich brown gravy bubbling up the sides of the buttery mashed potatoes.

beef, chestnut, and brandy pies

Beef

5 tablespoons unsalted butter

2¾ pounds chuck steak, trimmed of fat
and diced

4–6 strips bacon, diced

2 onions, peeled, halved, and thinly
sliced

3 garlic cloves, peeled and
finely chopped

6 tablespoons brandy

1 tablespoon all-purpose flour

1 cup red wine

1 cup beef stock or water

1 bay leaf

1 small bunch of fresh thyme,
tied with string

sea salt, black pepper

1½ cups (7 ounces) cooked and peeled
chestnuts, quartered

2 tablespoons mushroom ketchup
(optional)

On Top

3¼ pounds potatoes, peeled and halved
or quartered if large

1½ pounds parsnips, peeled and cut
into pieces

10 tablespoons unsalted butter, diced

Serves 6

Heat 3 tablespoons of butter in a large cast-iron baking dish over medium-high heat. Add some of the cubed meat, leaving plenty of space between the pieces, and sear on all sides (without seasoning), then remove and cook the remainder in the same fashion, adding more butter if necessary. Add the bacon to the pan and fry for several minutes until lightly colored, stirring occasionally, then add the onion and continue to fry for 5–7 minutes, until really golden, stirring now and then. Add the garlic just before the end.

Return the meat to the pan and give everything a stir, then flambé with the brandy. I find it easiest to heat a little at a time in a ladle over a gas flame, swirling it around until it ignites, and then gradually pour it on top. Once the flames have died down stir in the flour, then add the wine and stock or water, the herbs, and a little seasoning (bearing in mind that the bacon will do a lot of the work). Bring to a boil, then cover and cook over very low heat for 1–1½ hours, or until the meat is tender and sitting in a rich golden gravy. Stir occasionally, especially towards the end, to prevent it from catching on the bottom. Discard the herbs and stir in the chestnuts and mushroom ketchup if using, then transfer to a bowl, cover, and leave to cool.

Bring a large pot of salted water to a boil, add the potatoes and parsnips, bring back to a simmer, and cook until tender. Drain them and leave for a minute or two to steam dry, then pass through a food mill or a sieve back into the pan. Add the butter, and season to taste. Divide the pie filling between six 2-cup ovenproof dishes, and smooth the mashed potato on top. Using the end of a teaspoon, make indentations in the potato, then leave to cool. The pies can be frozen at this point, otherwise cover and chill until required. Cook them (defrosted) for 40–45 minutes in an oven preheated to 350°F until the pies are golden on top, and the gravy is bubbling at the sides.

The treat here is the crisp slivers of bread on top of the casserole, which are slightly soggy where they've soaked up the gravy underneath. The lengthy list of ingredients that go to making special-occasion casseroles belies their ease of making. Like any other, this is all tied up within a twenty-minute flurry at the start of cooking. Look out for Chantenay carrots; a fat baby carrot, they're perfect casserole material.

venison carbonade

4 tablespoons unsalted butter,
   plus extra for spreading
3 onions, peeled, halved, and sliced
2 garlic cloves, peeled and smashed
2 pounds stewing venison, diced
2 tablespoons all-purpose flour
sea salt, black pepper
1 cup Guinness
2 cups beef stock
½ pound baby carrots, peeled
2 sticks of celery, trimmed and sliced
about 10 sprigs of fresh thyme,
   tied into a bunch
2 bay leaves
2 teaspoons light brown sugar
1 teaspoon red wine vinegar
approx. 20 thin slices of French bread
   (about ½ baguette)
Dijon mustard

Serves 4–6

Preheat the oven to 350°F. Melt half the butter in a large cast-iron baking dish over medium heat, add the onions, and fry for 8–10 minutes until golden, stirring occasionally, adding the garlic just before the end, then move them to a bowl. Toss the venison with the flour and some seasoning in a bowl, and sear it in two batches, adding half the remaining butter with each one. You may need to turn the heat up towards the end.

Return the onions to the baking dish, pour in the Guinness and beef stock, and add the carrots, celery, herbs, sugar, vinegar, and some seasoning. Bring the liquid to a boil, then cover and cook in the oven for 1½ hours.

Remove the baking dish from the oven and turn the temperature up to 400°F. Season the stew to taste. Butter the slices of French bread on one side, and spread with mustard on the other. Arrange these so they overlap, mustard side down, in rows on top of the baking dish, and return it to the oven for another 30–40 minutes, until they are golden and crisp. Serve immediately. If making the dish in advance, reheat it on the stove top, and finish with the bread slices just before serving.

A homemade steak and kidney pie makes a special dinner, and I often make up the filling and the pastry in advance and freeze them. It's a great one for New Year's Eve, as well as for day two or three of the festivities when you still have a full house but the enthusiasm for cooking yet another meal may be waning. Dish it up with a big bowl of mashed potatoes, and a down-to-earth veggie such as cabbage that will keep it in the right rustic vein.

steak and guinness pie with wild mushrooms

5 tablespoons vegetable oil

2 leeks, trimmed and sliced

1 celery heart, sliced

2¼ pounds chuck steak, trimmed of fat and diced

2 heaping tablespoons all-purpose flour

½ cup medium sherry

1 cup Guinness or other stout

1 cup beef stock

1 bay leaf

3 sprigs of fresh thyme

sea salt, black pepper

9 ounces lambs' kidneys, fat and ducts removed, sliced

10½ ounces (5 cups) wild mushrooms, e.g. porcini, or flavorsome cultivated ones, picked over and sliced

1¼ pounds shortcrust pastry

1 egg yolk, mixed with 1 tablespoon milk

Serves 6

Heat 2 tablespoons of the oil in a large saucepan. Add the leeks and celery and cook gently over low heat for about 8 minutes, until soft and just beginning to color, stirring occasionally, then put in a bowl. You will need to sear the meat in two batches. Turn the heat up, add half the meat to the pan, and toss to sear and color it, then remove it and cook the remainder. It's worth taking your time doing this, to ensure the meat colors properly, as this will help flavor the gravy. Return the meat and vegetables to the pan, sprinkle the flour on top, and stir to coat everything thoroughly. Pour in the sherry, Guinness, and beef stock, stirring well into a smooth sauce, and add the herbs and some seasoning. Bring the liquid to a simmer, cover, and braise over a low heat for 1–1½ hours or until the meat is tender, stirring occasionally, especially towards the end.

While it's cooking, heat a tablespoon of oil in a frying pan over high heat, add the kidneys, toss to sear them, and then remove from the pan. Heat another tablespoon of oil, add half the mushrooms, and cook, tossing them, until they are soft and starting to color. Add them to the kidneys and cook the remainder in the same way. Once the meat is cooked, remove the herbs and check the seasoning, stir in the mushrooms and kidneys, and leave to cool. You can now freeze the filling, or use it fresh.

Preheat the oven to 400°F. Thinly roll out two-thirds of the pastry on a floured work surface and line a deep 2- to 3-quart pie dish. Don't worry if you have to mend the pastry in places, it won't show once it's cooked. Transfer the filling into the pie and paint the rim above it with egg wash. Thinly roll the remaining third of the pastry to fit the surface. Lay the pastry for the lid on top of the pie and trim the edges, leaving ½ inch for shrinkage. Now press the edges together using a fork. Paint the surface with the egg wash. Roll out some of the pastry trimmings and cut out some stars to decorate the pie. Paint them with the egg wash, bake the pie for 45–50 minutes until nice and golden, and serve immediately.

My family are all retro diehards. I can spend hours dreaming up imaginative uses for leftover turkey and ham, only to arrive back at this dish—slivers of meat in a rich creamy white sauce made with the turkey stock, with buttery mashed potatoes on top. On the side? Well, frozen peas of course. And the real joy is that you can prepare it lock, stock, and barrel well in advance and pop it into the oven forty minutes before you want to eat.

retro turkey and ham pie

Filling

4 tablespoons unsalted butter

½ cup all-purpose flour

½ cup dry white wine

1 cup turkey stock

1¼ cups sour cream

1 heaping teaspoon Dijon mustard

sea salt, black pepper

1 tablespoon peanut or vegetable oil

9 ounces (4¼ cups) chestnut or wild
    mushrooms, picked over and sliced
    if necessary

1¼ pounds shredded leftover turkey

½ cup diced ham

2 tablespoons fresh tarragon leaves

Mashed Potatoes

3¼ pounds potatoes, peeled
    and halved if large

1 cup sour cream

3½ tablespoons unsalted butter

2 large egg yolks

Serves 6

To make the sauce, melt the butter in a medium-size non-stick saucepan, add the flour, and allow the roux to seethe for a minute. Very gradually work in the wine, the turkey stock, then the sour cream, mustard, and a little seasoning. Bring to a boil, stirring constantly, and simmer over very low heat for 10 minutes, stirring occasionally. If any butter separates out simply stir vigorously until it is reincorporated.

At the same time heat the oil in a large frying pan, add the mushrooms, season and fry, cooking off any liquid that is given out until they are lightly colored.

Taste the sauce to check the seasoning, then fold in the turkey, ham, mushrooms, and tarragon leaves. Transfer the mixture to a 14-inch oval gratin dish or other ovenproof dish with a 2½ quart capacity that affords a large crispy surface. Leave to cool before you smooth the potato on top.

Bring a large pot of salted water to a boil and cook the potatoes until they are tender. Drain them into a sieve or colander and leave the surface moisture to evaporate for a minute or two. Pass through a food mill or a sieve back into the pot. Heat the sour cream with the butter and some seasoning and beat this into the potato, followed by the egg yolks. Smooth the potato over the top of the turkey, forking the surface into furrows.

Preheat the oven to 400°F and bake the pie for 40 minutes, until crusty and golden on top. You can cover and chill the pie until required, for up to 48 hours. In this case it may need a little longer in the oven.

Here a crispy layer of thinly sliced potatoes takes the place of the usual mashed, with haddock in parsley sauce below.

boulangère fish pie

2 pounds haddock fillets (skin on)
1 cup whole milk
sea salt, black pepper
4 tablespoons unsalted butter
½ cup all-purpose flour
½ cup white wine
½ cup heavy cream
1 heaping teaspoon Dijon mustard
6 salted anchovy fillets, sliced
½ cup finely chopped fresh flat-leaf
  parsley
10½ ounces cooked and peeled
  jumbo shrimp
2 pounds potatoes, peeled
2 tablespoons peanut or
  vegetable oil

Serves 6

Place the haddock fillets skin side down in a large saucepan, cutting them to fit. Pour the milk in, season with black pepper, and bring to a boil. Cover with a lid, leaving a gap for the steam to escape, and cook on low heat for 4 minutes. Strain the cooking liquid into a bowl, and, once the fish is cool enough to handle, flake it as coarsely as possible, discarding the skin. If any additional liquid is given out beyond this point throw it away.

To make the béchamel, melt the butter in a medium-size non-stick saucepan, add the flour, and allow the roux to seethe for a minute. Very gradually work in the wine, the fish cooking liquid, and the cream, then stir in the mustard and the anchovies. Bring to a boil, stirring constantly, and simmer over very low heat for 10 minutes, stirring occasionally. If any butter separates out simply stir vigorously until it is reincorporated. Taste to check the seasoning, then stir in the parsley and fold in the haddock and shrimp. Transfer the fish to a 14-inch oval gratin dish or other ovenproof dish with a 2½ quart capacity that affords a large surface. Cover the surface with plastic wrap and leave the fish to cool, which will help prevent the potatoes from sinking in. You can prepare the pie to this point several hours in advance, or the day beforehand if you are confident about the freshness of your fish, in which case chill it.

Preheat the oven to 400°F. Slice the potatoes as finely as possible using a sharp knife, discarding the ends. Toss the potato slices in a large bowl with the oil and some seasoning and arrange them on top of the fish, overlapping like roof tiles, but quite tightly as you only want one layer. If using an oval gratin dish, start at the outside and then work inwards to the center. Gently press down with your hands to level them. Bake the pie for about 40 minutes until the potatoes are crisp and golden at the edges, and tender.

An oldie but goodie, based on Jane Grigson's famed "salmon in pastry," which in turn was based on a dish served many years ago at the Hole in the Wall in Bath, England. It's one of those strange but magical combinations that has the air of being special every time you try it. If it's a "blow the cholesterol" occasion, you could make a sleek little sauce with sour cream, a dash of Dijon mustard, and some chopped leafy herbs such as dill, chives, and flat-leaf parsley.

salmon en croûte with stem ginger and currants

7 tablespoons unsalted butter, softened
4 knobs of stem ginger in syrup,
  finely chopped
3 tablespoons currants
finely grated zest of 1 lemon, plus a
  couple of squeezes of juice
1 tablespoon finely chopped
  fresh tarragon leaves
1 shallot, peeled and finely chopped
sea salt, black pepper
2¾ pounds salmon fillet
  (skinned weight), in one piece
13 ounces puff pastry
1 egg yolk, blended with
  1 teaspoon water

Serves 6

Blend the butter in a bowl with the ginger, currants, lemon zest and juice, tarragon, shallot, and some seasoning. Cut the salmon fillet in half. Season both sides of each piece, then spread half the butter over the top of one piece, sandwich with the other, and spread the remaining butter on top of this.

Thinly roll out the pastry on a lightly floured work surface, and place the salmon in the center, buttered side down. Trim the long edges so they are just large enough to enclose the salmon, then seal the parcel, painting the rim of the pastry with egg wash to secure it. Trim the ends, paint these with egg wash, and fold in to secure. Place the parcel the right way up, and use the pastry trimmings to decorate it with leaves or a fish, securing them to the top with egg wash. Now paint the top all over with egg wash. The parcel can be made up to half a day in advance, in which case cover and chill it until required.

Preheat the oven to 425°F and bake the pie for about 40 minutes. Serve in slices.

gorgeous birds

Part of our French country Christmas as a family involves wandering down the lane and being heckled by our neighbors' turkeys as we pass. An elderly farming couple, they are typical of rural smallholders in Normandy who will rear a few turkeys in the run-up to Christmas. These birds lead as free a life as you could hope for, wandering from the shelter of a barn to the grass outside. They have rekindled my faith in the potential of turkey; at its finest the flesh is the palest pink, finely grained, succulent, and almost gamey. Buy carefully and there is no reason why Christmas dinner should ever offer up less—today's well-reared bronze and rarer black turkeys are a world apart from the oversized birds bred for speed of growth that I grew up with.

Breed is not all, mind you, the cook plays a part. Going back a few years, the fashion for roasting a turkey was either to put it in to cook the night before, or to set the alarm for an hour or two before the cock crowed. Either way it was hours more than was required, so trust me on the timings here even if they do seem on the slim side of those you are accustomed to. Roasting the bird breast down will also make all the difference to keeping it succulent, allowing the fat and juices to trickle down into the flesh and baste it as it cooks.

For those who prefer to veer from the normal roast turkey, why not try pot-roast turkey, where the cooking juices keep the bird in fine succulent form and give you a ready-made gravy at the end? And if not turkey, there are any number of other birds that will be just as Christmassy dressed for the occasion, but that accommodate smaller numbers. Gatherings of two, three, and four will almost certainly do better with a duck, a partridge, or even a goose. My ideal size of turkey is one up from that demanded by the occasion itself, and renders just enough left over for a turkey and ham pie, and of course some lovely soup.

By this stage of the game, the only thing you really want to know is how to get Christmas dinner on the table with the minimum of possible fuss. It's hard enough juggling the trimmings without doing anything fancy with the bird. So this is your "quick set-up guide." However, if you do want to take the fancy route, the quatre épices butter provides a custom-made Christmas scent that gently infuses the turkey flesh as it cooks, while the butter bastes the breast—and it can be done in advance!

roast turkey

1 x 11- to 12-pound turkey
2 tablespoons unsalted butter, softened
sea salt, black pepper

Serves 8–10

the quick set-up guide

Preheat the oven to 425°F. Stuff the turkey (see page 96–97), then rub the butter over the bird and season. Set the turkey breast side down in a large roasting pan. Protect the wings and legs with foil to prevent them from drying out. Place the turkey in the oven and roast for 30 minutes, then turn down to 400°F and continue roasting for the times suggested below (to include the 30 minutes).

Baste periodically with the juices in the roasting pan. About 30–45 minutes before the bird is cooked, turn it breast up, removing the foil, so that it can brown. To check if the bird is cooked through, insert a skewer into the thickest part of the flesh (the thigh). The juices should run out clear. If not, give the bird another 10 minutes, then check again. Remove the turkey to a carving plate and leave it to rest for around 20 minutes while you make the gravy (see page 102–105). Carve the turkey and serve with the gravy.

roasting times

For a bird up to 11 pounds, allow 15 minutes per pound.
For a bird over 11 pounds, allow 13 minutes per pound.

roast turkey quatre épices

5–6 tablespoons unsalted butter, softened
½ teaspoon each ground cinnamon,
   cloves, nutmeg, allspice
sea salt, black pepper
a bunch of fresh thyme or rosemary
zest of 1 lemon, removed with
   a potato peeler

Blend the butter with the spices and some seasoning in a bowl. Starting at the neck end, slip your fingers beneath the skin to loosen it over each breast. Spread the spiced butter underneath the skin over the breasts and pat the skin back into place, spreading the butter out evenly. Put the herbs and lemon into the cavity. Cook as before.

This makes for a supremely succulent bird, and the gravy is part of the package, which is one less thing to worry about. By roasting the turkey on top of the giblets, you even have their lovely savor too. Use "extra thick" foil for this, as it's less likely to tear or pierce.

pot-roast turkey with port gravy

1 lemon

3–4 tablespoons unsalted butter, softened

1 tablespoon sliced fresh sage leaves

1 tablespoon fresh thyme leaves

sea salt, black pepper

1 x approx. 11-pound turkey, with giblets (reserve the livers for another time)

1 onion, peeled and sliced

vegetable oil

¾ cup port

Serves 8–10

roasting times

For a bird up to 11 pounds, allow 15 minutes per pound, plus 10 minutes over.

For a bird over 11 pounds, allow 13 minutes per pound, plus 20 minutes over.

Preheat the oven to 400°F. Finely grate the lemon zest. Blend the butter, herbs, lemon zest, and some seasoning in a bowl. Starting at the neck end of the turkey, slip your fingers beneath the skin to loosen it over each breast, breaking the membrane between them. Insert the herb butter, dividing it between the breasts, and pat the skin to spread the butter out evenly. Roll the lemon on the work surface, prick it all over, and pop it into the neck cavity, tucking the flap of skin underneath.

Place the turkey on top of the giblets and the onion in a large roasting pan that holds the bird quite snugly. Lightly oil the turkey and season it with salt and pepper. Pour 2 cups of water into the base of the pan and cover with foil. The pan should be airtight, leaving enough room for the bird to stretch as it cooks without piercing the foil. Basically, you will need to pleat several lengths of foil together, with enough spare to tuck underneath the pan. If the foil isn't totally secured, the steam created inside will lift it off during roasting. Roast for 30 minutes, then turn the oven down to 350°F and continue to roast for the times suggested below.

Forty-five minutes before the end of cooking, remove the foil. There should still be a good pool of liquid in the base, but if not, add a little more water. Add the port, baste, and return the bird to the oven to brown. To check if the bird is cooked through, insert a skewer into the thickest part of the thigh—the juices should run out clear. If not, and if they appear bloody or pink, give the bird another 15 minutes, then check again.

Transfer the turkey to a carving plate to rest for 20 minutes, loosely covering it with foil. Simmer the gravy on the stove until it tastes well-balanced, then pass it through a sieve into a gravy boat. Add any juices given out on carving the bird.

Turkey breasts come off the bone and on, when they are known as a crown roast. I like to buy mine boned and rolled and to stuff it myself, as here, where the leeks provide a buttery succulence, and the porcini work their perfumed magic, and you get crispy bacon on the outside to boot.

stuffed roast turkey breast with cranberry gravy

Stuffing

8 tablespoons unsalted butter

5 leeks (1¼ pounds trimmed weight),
    sliced

sea salt, black pepper

approx. 1¾ cups dried porcini, soaked
    in 1 cup boiling water for 30 minutes

2 tablespoons chopped fresh
    flat-leaf parsley

finely grated zest of 1 lemon,
    plus a squeeze of juice

3 ounces unsweetened brioche

2 medium egg yolks

1 cup rich chicken stock

Turkey and Gravy

1 x 3¼- to 3½-pound turkey breast,
    boned and rolled

5 strips of bacon

sea salt, black pepper

6 tablespoons port

1 tablespoon cranberry sauce

Serves 6

To make the stuffing* melt 3½ tablespoons of the butter in a large frying pan over medium heat, add the leeks, season them, and cook gently for 12–15 minutes until soft and lightly colored, stirring occasionally. Transfer them to a bowl. Drain and finely chop the porcini, reserving the liquid. Stir the mushrooms into the leeks together with the parsley, lemon zest, and juice. Leaving the crusts on the brioche, reduce it to fine crumbs in a food processor and stir these into the stuffing. Add the egg yolks and blend using a wooden spoon. The stuffing can be prepared to this point several hours in advance, in which case cover and set it aside in a cool place.

Preheat the oven to 400°F. Snip the string binding the turkey breast and slip the ties off. Lay the bacon strips in a row on the chopping board about 1 inch apart, and lay the turkey breast skin down on top. Open the pocket of the breast and stuff with about a third of the stuffing. Bring the bacon slices up around the sides and tie it up again, wrapping a piece of string around each strip of bacon to secure it. Season it on both sides with salt and pepper and place skin side up in a roasting dish that holds it snugly. Dot with 3½ tablespoons of the butter, pour the reserved mushroom soaking liquor on top, and roast for 18 minutes per pound (including the weight of the stuffing). Baste the joint a couple of times in the course of roasting, adding a drop more water or chicken stock to the roasting dish towards the end if the juices get too syrupy.

Shape the remaining stuffing into balls the size of a plum and arrange in a shallow ovenproof dish, spaced about ½ inch apart. Pour half the chicken stock into the base of the baking dish to a depth of ¼ inch, dot the stuffing balls with the remaining tablespoon of butter, and roast for 30–35 minutes, until lightly golden (i.e. putting them into the oven about 10 minutes before the turkey is ready to allow for it resting).

Once the turkey is cooked, transfer the joint and any stuffing on the bottom of the dish to a warm carving plate, loosely cover with foil and leave to rest for 20 minutes. Skim any excess fat from the roasting dish, add the port, and simmer to reduce by half, scraping up all the sticky bits. Stir in the cranberry sauce and once the jelly has melted blend in the rest of the stock. Simmer for a few minutes, until it tastes nice and rich. Taste and add a little more seasoning if necessary. Carve the turkey, adding any juices to the gravy.

*If you prefer you could make all the stuffing into balls to cook outside the turkey, in which case dot with 2 tablespoons of butter and pour 1 cup of stock on top.

roast goose with prune and apple stuffing

A plump roast goose with its crackly parchment-crisp skin and succulent dark flesh goes unsurpassed. I enjoy it best stuffed with prunes and apples, and served with some small crispy potatoes (see page 80) and a pile of watercress or other salad greens. Maybe the luxury of a bread sauce thrown in, but no more than that. In fact it's so easy to prepare I always stand around thinking I must have forgotten something.

Although goose has a reputation for being leaner than a turkey, a 10-pound bird does nicely for six, and the average oven will accommodate up to at least 12 pounds. One of the great joys in roasting a goose is the copious golden fat given off, which makes for superlative roasted and sautéd potatoes. Any fat that comes separately with the giblets, or that you remove from the bird's cavity, can also be put to use. Gently heat it in a small frying pan or saucepan, strain, and bottle it in a wide-necked jar. It keeps almost indefinitely in the fridge.

Whereas we usually base gravy on the roasting juices in the bottom of the pan, with goose it is better to play it safe and prepare it using the giblets. You can include the goose liver in this line-up, though there again it's such a delicacy you may like to keep it for a treat the next day. The gravy can also be made in advance and reheated.

Stuffing

1¾ cups pitted prunes

1 cup port

2 tablespoons unsalted butter

1 pound Bramley apples, peeled,
    cored, and diced

1 tablespoon superfine sugar

Goose

1 x 10 pound goose, with giblets

peanut oil

sea salt, black pepper

watercress to serve 6

1 x quantity of bread sauce,
    optional (see page 101)

Gravy

½ cup port

1 teaspoon all-purpose flour, sifted

1½ cups giblet stock (see page 104)

Serves 6

To make the stuffing, place the prunes in a small saucepan with the port. Bring to a boil, then simmer over low heat for 15–20 minutes until all but a tablespoon of syrupy liquid remains, stirring towards the end. At the same time, melt the butter in a large frying pan over medium heat, add the apples, and sauté for about 5 minutes, stirring frequently, until lightly colored and just beginning to lose their shape. Sprinkle the sugar on top and cook for a minute or so longer until you have the beginnings of an apple sauce, with whole pieces still evident. Combine the prunes and residual syrup with the apples in a bowl, cover with a plate or plastic wrap, and leave to cool. Chill if preparing more than a few hours in advance of using.

Preheat the oven to 400°F. Place a rack in a roasting pan that contains ¼ inch of water in the bottom (see page 9). Place two large sheets of foil on top of the rack, overlapping widthways, and pierce so that the fat can drain through. Remove any surplus fat at the entrance to the body cavity of the goose. Leaving the bird trussed, spoon the stuffing into the cavity, pushing it well back.

Rub the goose all over with oil and season. Prick the skin and fat gland under each wing. Cover the legs with some of the surplus fat and wrap them in foil. Place the goose breast side up on the foil and wrap it into a parcel.

Cook the goose for 16–17 minutes per pound, therefore roughly 2½ hours for a 10-pound goose. Roast for 30 minutes, then turn the oven down to 350°F. A third of the way into cooking, unwrap and remove the foil, leaving the legs covered. Drain off any excess fat, reserving it for later, turn the goose breast down, and roast for another third of the total time. Turn the goose breast up again, draining off any more excess fat, and roast for the remainder of the cooking time. Transfer the goose to a warm serving plate, loosely cover with foil, and leave to rest for 30 minutes.

Skim any excess fat from the giblet roasting pan, add the port, and simmer on the stove until well reduced. Stir in the flour, dispersing any lumps with the back of the spoon, and once this is simmering, gradually stir in the stock. Simmer the gravy long and hard enough for it to amalgamate into a smooth sauce. Taste and season if necessary. Pass through a sieve into a gravy boat to serve. Carve the goose and serve with a spoonful of the stuffing and a pile of watercress. Serve the gravy and any bread sauce separately at the table.

A classically gorgeous scenario of ingredients that go together hand in hand. Under normal circumstances, two people will make light work of a duck, but eaten with blood sausage it will spread to four. I usually serve small baked potatoes with this, but sautéed potatoes are just as good. I would make a big jug of "extra gravy" (see page 102) to go with this. Duck benefits from a long slow roasting, the surest way of ensuring crisp golden skin, and farmed duck is preferable to wild here.

roast duck with blood sausage and apple

Duck

1 x 5½-pound duck, oven-ready
sea salt
a handful each of fresh sage leaves,
    oregano sprigs, and thyme sprigs

Dressing

2 eating apples, peeled, cored, and sliced
8 x ½-inch slices of blood sausage
watercress to serve 4

Serves 4

Preheat the oven to 350°F. Prick the duck skin all over with a skewer and generously rub with salt. Stuff the cavity of the duck with the herbs. Place the duck breast side up on a rack within a roasting pan and roast for 1 hour (see page 9). Drain the fat into a bowl, turn the oven down to 300°F, and roast for a further 1½ hours, draining it a second time halfway through. Transfer the duck to a warm plate, loosely cover it with foil, and leave to rest for 20 minutes.

While the duck is resting, heat 2 tablespoons of the duck fat in a large frying pan over a high heat and sauté the apples for about 6 minutes, turning them now and then until golden on both sides. Transfer them to a warm plate, add another tablespoon of duck fat to the pan, and color the blood sausage slices for about 1 minute on either side. Serve the roast duck with the blood sausage and apple, some gravy, and a pile of watercress.

The traditional line-up for grouse of bread sauce, buttery crumbs, and watercress is just as good with other game birds. A grey partridge for me steals the show with its tender gaminess. It does one for one, which makes it ideal when it's just two, three, or four of you. I would make a big jug of "extra gravy" (see page 102) to go with this.

partridge that thinks it's a grouse

Partridge

4 grey-leg partridges, oven-ready,
    untrussed
4 tablespoons unsalted butter, softened
sea salt, black pepper
8 strips of bacon

Dressing and Crumbs

10–11 tablespoons unsalted butter
2½ cups fresh white breadcrumbs
1 x quantity of bread sauce (see
    page 101)
redcurrant jam or other game sauce
    to serve
watercress to serve 4

Serves 4

Preheat the oven to 400°F. Smear the birds with the butter, season them with pepper and the tiniest pinch of salt, then wrap two strips of bacon around each bird, one securing the legs. Place in a roasting pan about ½ inch apart and roast for 30 minutes, basting halfway through. Transfer the birds to a warm serving plate to rest for 10 minutes. If you want your bacon extra crispy, unwrap the bacon strips and lay these in another small baking dish, then return this to the oven to crisp for a few minutes while the bird is resting.

To make the crumbs, melt the butter in a large frying pan over medium heat and once it is sizzling nicely add the breadcrumbs and fry, stirring frequently, until they are evenly gold—this may take up to 15 minutes, depending on how fresh the crumbs are. Spread them in a thin layer on a double layer of paper towel to drain for a few minutes, then transfer to a bowl. They can be made up to about an hour in advance, but keep them somewhere warm in the kitchen so they remain feathery light and the butter doesn't set.

Just before eating, gently re-warm the bread sauce, spoon it into a bowl, and serve separately at the table with the game crumbs and the redcurrant jelly. Accompany each partridge with the bacon and a small bunch of watercress.

lavish main courses

The proper feasting in our house begins on Christmas Eve. Traditionally we roast a whole turbot, which is as easy as it is spectacular. In France, where we always spend Christmas, seafood is a big part of the *reveillon*, the traditional Christmas Eve dinner, so fishmongers are every bit as lavishly decked out as the butcher, the slab laid out with beautiful specimens. Turbot is an obvious treat, but a whole sole won't let you down and neither will a large halibut or two. While for those who want to avoid turkey and its ilk on the day, a rib of beef or filet mignon "en croute" are equally lavish.

A ham at Christmas is for most as essential to the celebrations as the tree and the turkey. As such it is possessed of a culture of its own; the pickles, mustardy sauces, and spiced fruits that go hand in hand, and the sandwiches that can be made with the proceeds, are a treat to be anticipated in the days that follow. Plan it right and it can span several days, first eaten hot with a parsley sauce, and thereafter cold. The third delight is the stock left over from boiling the ham or made with the proceeds of the bone on which it was cooked—with the addition of a few modest vegetables, some pearl barley, and strips of ham it can be turned into a warming feast.

The most popular cut of gammon (an uncooked ham) is the leg, which comes on the bone, or boned and rolled. The latter can be obtained in almost any size, though a 4½-pound joint will do nicely for eight people and just fit your biggest pot, and should promise to be beautifully succulent. A knuckle-end gammon joint (half leg on the bone) is good for ten plus. Good butchers, some of whom cure their own gammons, will be able to advise on whether you need to soak your gammon overnight; if however you are buying from a supermarket I would recommend soaking the gammon as a matter of course. As to unsmoked or smoked, it's a question of taste, and your preference should steer the course.

This juicy joint of ham with a sticky glaze can be served hot, with a creamy gravy made with the basting juices, but as ever it's just as good cold. Ham, like turkey, is a dinner of several lives, and it seems a shame not to cook a joint that will give you plenty to carve in the days to come. Gammon from the middle cut of leg can come up wide and thin, so for ease of carving aim for a joint 6 inches long and about 5 inches in diameter.

earl grey ham

1 x 5½- to 6¾-pound unsmoked
    gammon (uncooked ham), boned
    and rolled
3 outer sticks of celery, trimmed
    and sliced
2 carrots, trimmed and sliced
1 leek, trimmed and sliced
2 bay leaves
1½ tablespoons wholegrain mustard
¼ cup dark brown sugar
approx. 1¾ to 2 cups strong
    Earl Grey tea
1¼ cups sour cream

Serves 8–10

Consult your butcher, and if necessary soak the gammon in cold water overnight, then drain. Place the gammon in a large pot, cover with cold water, and bring to a boil. Discard the water and start again with fresh water to cover, this time adding the chopped vegetables and bay leaves. Bring to a boil, and maintain at a gentle simmer, adding boiling water if necessary. Calculate the cooking time at 40 minutes per 2¼ pounds, subtracting 35 minutes for glazing it in the oven. So a 6¾-pound joint will need 1 hour 25 minutes boiling.

Preheat the oven to 425°F. Transfer the ham from the pot to a cutting board using two forks. Remove any string and paper around it, and pull or cut off the rind if present. Slash the fat at ¾-inch intervals in a crisscross pattern, without going down as far as the meat. It is a good idea to skewer the opening where the bone was with a couple of metal skewers, one going each way, so the ham doesn't unravel in the oven.

Brush the fat with the mustard, then press the sugar on top. Place the ham fat side up in a roasting dish and pour 1¾ cups of the tea into the base. Roast for 30–35 minutes, until the glaze is sticky and caramelized. Baste the ham halfway through, adding a little more tea if you think it's reducing too quickly—there should be a pool of rich golden juices at the end. Transfer the ham to a serving plate, and leave to rest for 20 minutes. Add the sour cream to the juices and simmer until rich and amalgamated. Remove the skewers, carve, and serve the ham with the sauce. You can also reheat the sliced ham in the sauce at a later date, a useful one for all those teenagers traipsing back from a night out.

This is a lovely sticky aromatic glaze that makes a change from the norm, and the pan juices can be eked out, with the addition of a little cream, to give you a rich sauce for serving it hot. You could also add some finely chopped parsley.

sherry and quince-glazed ham

1 x 7¾-pound knuckle-end smoked gammon (uncooked ham) joint on the bone

⅔ cup quince paste or jelly (membrillo)

3 tablespoons wholegrain mustard

¼ cup medium sherry

approx. 40 cloves

¾–1 cup heavy cream

Serves 10

Consult your butcher, and if necessary soak the gammon in cold water overnight, then drain.

Preheat the oven to 375°F. Try to use the broadest width of foil. Tear off a long sheet, large enough to envelop the gammon, allowing plenty of air within the package to circulate. If the foil isn't wide enough, pleat the edges of two or three lengths together to create one large piece. Place the gammon on top, bring the long sides together, fold to seal them, then do the same with the sides. Place the gammon in a roasting dish. It needs to bake for 60 minutes per 2¼ pounds, so calculate it accordingly, subtracting 30 minutes for the final glazing. A 7¾-pound gammon will need to bake for about 3 hours prior to glazing.

Just before the end, gently heat the quince paste or jelly in a small saucepan, working it with a wooden spoon until it thins. Transfer to a bowl and blend in first the mustard and then the sherry. Remove the ham from the oven and turn the temperature up to 400°F. Unwrap the ham and remove the foil, then slice off the rind underneath the ham, which will have softened in the cooking juices, leaving behind as much of the fat as possible. Next carefully incise a long slit into the rind across the top without cutting into the fat—you can use scissors for this—and partly pull and partly cut the skin off. Use oven gloves or a kitchen towel to protect your hands from getting burned.

Glaze the top and sides of the ham as evenly as possible with the quince-sherry glaze. Slice the fat at 1-inch intervals with a crisscross pattern and insert cloves into the crosses on the fat.

Return the ham to the roasting dish and pour a ¼ inch of water into the base to prevent any glaze on the base from burning. Roast for 25–30 minutes, until the glaze is golden and dry, checking it halfway through and adding a little more water if necessary. Transfer the ham to a warm serving plate, loosely cover with foil, and leave to rest for 30 minutes.

If serving the ham hot, skim the fat off the juices in the roasting dish, add ½ to 1 cup of water and simmer for a few minutes, scraping up the residue on the bottom of the pan, then add the cream and simmer for a few minutes longer. Add any juices given out on resting the ham. To serve, moisten the meat with just a couple of spoons of the sauce, which is quite rich.

If serving the ham cold, place it somewhere cool or unheated and leave to cool completely. A pantry makes the ideal environment for storing a cooked ham; basically it should be somewhere cool and slightly damp—a garage is an alternative. It will keep well for about a week, or if it has been sliced then 3 days. You can reheat slices of ham in the sauce in the days to follow. First skim off any fat that has risen to the surface of the sauce on chilling.

Turbot has beautifully sweet white milky flesh, and roasting it on the bone ensures it remains succulent. Substituting sole or halibut works well too. Any potato of choice will be good here, buttery mashed or boiled with lots of salted butter, and a big green salad.

whole roasted fish

2 lemons, sliced, ends discarded

extra virgin olive oil

1 x approx. 4½-pound whole turbot, sole, or halibut

sea salt, black pepper

1 tablespoon soft fresh thyme leaves

1 tablespoon fresh rosemary

½ cup white wine

2 tablespoons unsalted butter

Serves 4

Preheat the oven to 425°F. Heat a large non-stick frying pan over medium-high heat. Brush the lemon slices with oil on both sides and sear these for about 1 minute each side, until colored. Score the flesh of both sides of the fish quite deeply, diagonally at 2-inch intervals. Season the slits well on both sides with salt and pepper, then stuff them with a pinch of the thyme and rosemary. Place the fish underside down in a roasting dish. Pour the wine on top, then top with the lemon slices and dot with the butter.

Roast for 30–35 minutes, until the flesh is just cooked. It should have lost its translucency and come away from the bone with ease.

This is a great centerpiece for any sit-down dinner or buffet. Because a rib of beef takes up most of the oven, I prefer to serve mashed rather than roasted potatoes—the Christmas champ on page 83 should do you proud. Jars of preserved grated fresh horseradish will stand in for fresh should it prove hard to find. Start by adding 2 tablespoons of horseradish to the sour cream, then taste and add more if you like.

roast rib of beef with horseradish sauce

Beef

1 x 3-bone rib of beef, oven-ready
½ teaspoon all-purpose flour, plus
   1 tablespoon
½ teaspoon English mustard powder
¼ cup port
½ teaspoon Dijon mustard
1½ cups beef stock
sea salt, black pepper

Sauce

1⅔ cups sour cream
2–3 tablespoons finely grated
   horseradish

Serves 6

Take your joint out of the fridge an hour before roasting to allow it to come to room temperature. Preheat the oven to 500°F (if your oven doesn't go that high, preheat it to its highest setting), and place the rib fat side up in a roasting pan that holds it snugly. Sift the ½ teaspoon of flour and the ½ teaspoon of mustard together, and dust this over the fat using a fine mesh sieve.

Roast the joint for 20 minutes, then turn the oven down to 400°F, allowing 12 minutes per 18 ounces for rare meat, and 15 minutes for medium rare. Baste the joint every 20–30 minutes.

To make the sauce, blend the sour cream and horseradish together and season with salt. Transfer to a clean bowl, cover, and chill until required.

Once cooked, transfer the joint to a serving plate and leave to rest for 20 minutes out of the oven, loosely covered with foil. Skim any excess fat off the roasting pan. Add the port and cook for a few minutes, scraping up all the sticky bits on the bottom, until well reduced. Stir in the Dijon mustard and the tablespoon of flour, then thin it with the beef stock and simmer for several minutes. Taste to check the seasoning, and pass through a sieve into a jug or bowl. Carve the roast and add any juices given out during the process of carving to the gravy. Serve the horseradish sauce separately at the table.

This remains the chicest party piece, hot or cold, and with the plethora of wild mushrooms available to us the results promise to be better than ever. Although filet mignon is undeniably expensive, you don't need quite as much as you would if eating another cut of steak. I would dish this up with some small crispy potatoes and mustard.

filet mignon en croûte

10½ ounces (5 cups) wild and
   cultivated mushrooms, picked
   over and trimmed
2 tablespoons unsalted butter
2 shallots, peeled and finely chopped
sea salt, black pepper
2 tablespoons chopped fresh
   flat-leaf parsley
a squeeze of lemon juice
1½-pound piece of filet mignon,
   trimmed of fat and sinew (ask
   your butcher for the thick end
   of the filet)
peanut oil
14 ounces puff pastry
3½–4 ounces cream cheese
1 scant tablespoon Dijon mustard,
   plus extra to serve
1 medium egg, beaten

Serves 4–6

Finely chop the mushrooms by hand into ¼-inch pieces. Melt the butter in a large frying pan over medium heat, add the shallots, and sweat for a few minutes until softened, stirring them occasionally. Add the mushrooms and some seasoning and continue to fry for another 5–6 minutes, until any juices given out have evaporated and they have started to color. Transfer them to a bowl, stir in the parsley and lemon juice, and leave to cool.

Heat another large frying pan over medium heat for several minutes. Brush the filet mignon all over with oil, season it, and sear for 1 minute on each side. Transfer to a plate and leave to cool.

Thinly roll out the pastry on a lightly floured work surface. Spread the cream cheese over the middle, to cover an area the size of the filet. Spread the mushrooms on top. Brush the top of the filet with the mustard and place, mustard-side down, on top of the mushrooms. Trim the pastry, allowing enough to parcel up the steak. Paint one of the long edges and both short sides with the beaten egg. Bring the long painted edge up over the other long edge, then tuck up the sides, trimming off any excess pastry and securing them with more egg wash. Place on a baking tray, sealed edges down, and use the trimmings to decorate the top of the pie, fixing them with the beaten egg. You can prepare the steak to this point a couple of hours in advance, cover, and chill it.

Preheat the oven to 475°F. Brush the croûte all over with the beaten egg and bake for 30 minutes, until golden. Leave to rest for 10 minutes, then carve into thick slices; don't worry if this seems rather messy. The end slices will be medium rare and the center ones rare. Accompany with extra mustard.

This rings the changes from the traditional Christmas palette, but is as festive as any other big roast, and anything pot-roasted makes for ease, with ready-made gravy that is so central to a pot of mashed or buttery potatoes. There is no need to forgo the crackling either. Ask your butcher to slice off the rind, so that the fat is evenly distributed between fat and skin, score, and roast it separately.

slow-roast pork shoulder with fennel and anchovies

Pork

1½ teaspoons fennel seeds,
  coarsely ground

⅓ teaspoon dried chile flakes

4½-pound boned and rolled shoulder
  of pork, rind removed and scored

sea salt

1 tablespoon extra virgin olive oil

½ bottle of white wine

1¼ cups chicken stock

7 salted anchovy fillets, sliced

3 garlic cloves, peeled and smashed

Fennel

4 fennel bulbs, shoots and outer sheath
  discarded, cut into thin wedges

½ cup chicken stock

½ cup white wine

2 tablespoons unsalted butter, diced

sea salt, black pepper

Serves 6

Preheat the oven to 300°F. Rub the fennel seeds and chile over the pork (don't worry about the ends), and season with salt. Heat the oil in a large frying pan over medium-high heat and brown the pork all over, then place it, fat side down, into a large cast-iron casserole. Add the wine, stock, anchovies, and garlic. Bring to a boil, then cover and place in the oven for 5 hours, turning it halfway through. At the same time, rub some salt into the pork skin, place it skin side up in a small roasting dish, and place in the oven.

Shortly before removing the pork from the oven, place all the ingredients for the fennel in a medium-size pot and bring to a boil. Cover the pot and cook for 30 minutes, until the fennel is meltingly tender, stirring halfway through, then drain.

When the 5 hours is up, transfer the pork to a plate to rest for 20 minutes, loosely covered with foil. Turn the oven up to 475°F to crisp the crackling while the meat is resting—it should turn pale, with small bubbles below the surface. Skim the fat off the roasting juices (you may find it easiest to pour these into a glass jug first and then return them to the pan). Simmer to reduce by about a third, until well flavored.

The meat should be meltingly tender and you should be able to just pull it apart with a fork and spoon. Serve with the juices, the fennel, and the crackling.

Squash come in many different shapes and sizes. Some are shaped like baby pumpkins and are ideal for stuffing. They are too pretty to miss on the Christmas table, and are patched with orange and green streaks. You could also stuff these the night before, and chill them overnight.

baked squash with wild mushrooms, apple, and chestnuts

2 squash (approx. 1½ pounds)
3½ tablespoons unsalted butter,
   plus extra to serve
3 shallots, peeled and finely chopped
2½ cups wild mushrooms, picked
   over and torn or sliced as necessary
1 apple, peeled, cored, and diced
sea salt, black pepper
⅔ cup cooked and peeled
   chestnuts, coarsely chopped
1 tablespoon fresh marjoram
   or thyme

Serves 6

Preheat the oven to 400°F. The squash need to stand level without rolling around, so if necessary slice off a sliver from each base. Cut off the tops and scoop out the seeds inside.

Melt the 3½ tablespoons of butter in a large frying pan over medium heat. Add the shallots and cook for a minute or two until softened, stirring occasionally, then add the mushrooms and apple and sauté for a few minutes longer, until the mushrooms are cooked and the apple is translucent and starting to color. Season, then add the chestnuts and marjoram or thyme, and cook for a minute longer.

Season the inside of the squash generously with salt and pepper and stuff with the mushroom and apple mixture, pressing it down well. Replace the lids, place the squash in a baking dish, and roast for 1 hour. To serve, scoop out the stuffing and the squash flesh. You may like to arrange this in a dish and dot with some butter to serve.

A lovely chicken curry is a winner around Christmas and New Year's. This one is mild and fragrant. I would serve it spooned over buttered spinach, accompanied by mini naan breads warmed in the oven for a few minutes, as well as a big dish of rice. Any luxury cocktail nut will do here, such as roasted almonds or salt and pepper cashews.

saffron butter chicken korma

3½ tablespoons unsalted butter

sea salt, black pepper

8 chicken thighs

2 onions, peeled, halved and
   thinly sliced

2 garlic cloves, peeled and
   finely chopped

¾ inch fresh ginger, peeled and
   finely chopped

2 medium-hot fresh red chiles

1 bay leaf

1 x 3-inch cinnamon stick

8 cloves

6 green cardamom pods, smashed
   with the bottom of a glass or a
   rolling pin

approx. 25 saffron filaments

1 teaspoon cornstarch

1 cup natural yogurt

chopped fresh cilantro and roasted
   pistachios to serve (optional)

a little chicken stock (if reheating)

Serves 4

Gently melt the butter in a small saucepan, skim off the surface foam, decant the clarified butter, and discard the milky solids below. Heat the clarified butter in a large cast-iron casserole over medium heat. Season the chicken thighs on both sides and color the flesh side for about 7 minutes until nicely golden, then turn and color the skin side for about another 7 minutes, again until nicely golden.

Transfer the chicken to a bowl, add the onions, garlic, ginger, chiles, bay leaf, and spices to the baking dish, and fry for another few minutes, until the onions are softened and starting to color. Return the chicken to the baking dish, placing it skin down and nestling it between the onions and spices. Cover the casserole and cook over a low heat for 30 minutes until the chicken is tender and comes away from the bone with ease.

Blend the cornstarch with a tablespoon of water in a medium-size bowl, then gradually blend in the yogurt. Transfer the chicken thighs to a serving dish and keep warm. Skim the fat off the cooking juices, stir in the yogurt and heat gently. The cornstarch will stabilize the sauce and prevent it from splitting if it boils. Taste, then spoon the sauce over the chicken thighs, and scatter the cilantro and pistachios on top if liked. You can pick out the whole spices as you eat. If you want to make it in advance and reheat it, you will probably need to thin the sauce with a little chicken stock.

all the trimmings

Who could possibly resist all the little side dishes that come with a roast, the trimmings as they are fondly known, however many or excessive they may be? It's the pick "n" mix that defines Christmas dinner: a fork piled with a small sprout, a dab of bread sauce, a sliver of bacon and sausage roll, followed by another of turkey with a little cranberry sauce and a morsel of stuffing. The potentially gorgeous forkfuls are endless, so let's not be too hard on ourselves for the lack of discipline in paring it down.

My own standard menu runs something like this: turkey with a sage and onion stuffing, sausage and chipolata rolls, roast potatoes, parsnips with Parmesan, sprouts with chestnuts, bread, and cranberry sauce, and a huge boat of gravy. Some people also like to serve ham at the same time as the turkey, though I usually wait until Boxing Day, the day after Christmas, for this one. I try to get well ahead on Christmas Eve, so there's no more than a couple of hours to be spent bringing it all together on the day, a peaceful time in the late afternoon when there's a lull in the presents and partying. We normally eat in the evening, around eight or nine, but I know lots of people who go for a late afternoon dinner around four o'clock. It's one of those meals you can serve any time that suits you from lunchtime onward.

And part of the excess is having lots of leftovers to carry you through the days to come. There is little more enjoyable the day after Christmas than grazing on a turkey that's been cooling in the pantry, with all the leftover trimmings. Turkey and bread sauce sandwiches are heaven, as is turkey with jellied gravy, or a cold chipolata and bacon roll dipped into the cranberry sauce. Next day's lunch takes care of itself. And once that's over, the turkey has yet another lease on life as a rich golden stock, and a retro turkey and ham pie. So think of roast turkey and "all the trimmings" as an investment, a promise of some feet-up time for the poor cook.

The best roasted potatoes are all crispy shell with just a little fluffy potato inside, which means cutting them small. As well as roasting them in butter, goose fat makes for fabulous results, and olive oil is a promise of super-crisp potatoes too. The main consideration is the potatoes themselves: use reliable varieties that will turn meltingly soft within, and have a lovely overall roasted flavor.

roasted potatoes

3½ pounds potatoes
8–10 tablespoons unsalted butter,
  melted
sea salt

Serves 6

Preheat the oven to 400°F. Peel and cut up your potatoes and reserve in a bowl of cold water. Bring a large pot of salted water to a boil. Add the potatoes to the pot and cook for 8 minutes. Drain the potatoes into a sieve and leave for a minute or two for the surface water to evaporate. Return them to the pot and roughly shake it from side to side, tossing them until they appear textured and floury on the surface.

Put them into a roasting pan, trickle the butter on top, and scatter with sea salt. Roast the potatoes for 1 hour and 15 minutes, turning them at least once during cooking. They should be evenly gold all over, the color of a potato chip.

When the call is for fries but you want something a little bit more sophisticated, these will get wolfed down regardless of what you serve them with. If you are increasing the quantity, however, you will need to use either a proportionately bigger roasting dish, or two, to ensure the fries color and crisp evenly.

oven-roasted fries with rosemary and thyme

2¾ pounds large potatoes, peeled
10 sprigs of fresh thyme
5 small sprigs of fresh rosemary
finely grated zest of 1 lemon, plus
   1 tablespoon lemon juice
2 tablespoons extra virgin olive oil
3 tablespoons unsalted butter
sea salt, black pepper

Serves 4–6

Preheat the oven to 400°F. Slice the potatoes lengthways ½ inch thick, then cut these slices into thick fries. Arrange them in a 15 x 10-inch roasting dish with the thyme, rosemary, and lemon zest. Drizzle with the olive oil and lemon juice, dot with the butter, and season. Cover with foil and roast for 25 minutes. Loosen the fries with a spatula and give them a stir, then roast uncovered for another 45–55 minutes until deliciously golden and caramelized, giving them another stir 10–15 minutes before the end.

A lovely lavish chestnut and mashed potato that can be dished up at any number of occasions over the festive period, with the turkey, or with roast ham, pork, or beef. It can be made in advance and gently reheated, which makes it perfect buffet material. Being prepared on the stove, it's also a good one for fancy joints and birds that are likely to dominate the oven, leaving no room for roasted potatoes.

christmas champ

2 pounds potatoes, peeled and cut up
9 ounces unsweetened chestnut purée
3 bunches of scallions
    (approx. 14 ounces), trimmed
7 tablespoons unsalted butter, plus
    a dollop to serve
1 cup heavy cream
sea salt, black pepper
freshly grated nutmeg

Serves 6

Bring a large pot of salted water to a boil and cook the potatoes for 20–25 minutes until tender. Drain, leave to steam dry, then press them through a foodmill back into the pot. Blend the chestnut purée in a food processor until it is really soft and creamy. Process this with the potato. At the same time as cooking the potatoes, cut the scallions into ½-inch slices including the green parts. Melt the butter in a medium or large saucepan over medium heat, and cook the scallions for about 5 minutes until it is soft and silky, stirring occasionally. Add the cream and season with salt, pepper, and nutmeg, bring to a simmer and cook for another few minutes until the mixture thickens.

Stir two-thirds of the cream and scallions into the purée and adjust the seasoning. If making this in advance, cover the surface of the mashed potato and the remaining sauce with plastic wrap and set aside. Just before serving, if necessary, gently reheat the purée and the reserved sauce. Spoon the potato purée into a serving bowl, pour the sauce on top, and turn it over a few times to loosely mix it in—most of the cream should remain on the surface. Make a well in the center and drop in the remaining dollop of butter.

This recipe was given to me by Jo Higgo, a friend who lives down the road from us in France, and I have never cooked parsnips any other way at Christmas since first tasting hers. The Parmesan cooks to a delicious toasty crisp that covers the parsnips.

parmesan-glazed parsnips

1¼ pounds parsnips, trimmed and
   peeled, halved lengthways, and cut
   into 2 shorter lengths
3½ tablespoons unsalted butter, melted
2½ tablespoons freshly grated
   Parmesan
black pepper

Serves 4–6

Heat the oven to 400°F and bring a large pot of salted water to a boil. Add the parsnips and cook for 8 minutes, then drain them in a colander and leave for a few minutes to steam dry. Place them in a roasting dish, drizzle with the butter, shake a little from side to side to coat them, then sprinkle the Parmesan on top, and season with pepper. Roast for 40–45 minutes, until the cheese is golden and crisp, basting and loosening them with a spatula halfway through. Serve immediately.

Brussels sprouts are a small oasis of green in an otherwise x-rated dinner. My family, shame on them, agree to eat one each, which makes for a lot of leftovers, but I'm not prepared to give up. Personally I think sprouts are a different vegetable when they're fried, the outside turning delicately crisp and sweet.

Don't worry about including the bacon bits if you're already doing bacon-wrapped chipolatas—simply fry the chestnuts with the sprouts. The vacummed packs or cans of cooked and peeled chestnuts come into their own here.

brussels sprouts with bacon and chestnuts

1½ pounds Brussels sprouts, base
  trimmed and outer leaves discarded
8 strips of bacon, diced
3½ ounces cooked and peeled
  chestnuts, sliced
3 tablespoons unsalted butter
sea salt, black pepper

Serves 6–8

Bring a large pot of salted water to a boil. Add the sprouts and cook for about 8 minutes, until just tender; larger sprouts will take longer accordingly. Drain in a colander.

Heat a large dry frying pan over medium heat, add the bacon, and cook for 7–8 minutes, stirring frequently, until crisp and golden. Use a slotted spoon to transfer to paper towels and allow the bacon to drain. Add the chestnuts to the pan and sauté in the bacon fat for several minutes, stirring frequently, until lightly golden. Transfer to a bowl and add the bacon.

Ten minutes before eating, melt the butter in a large frying pan over medium-high heat, add the sprouts, season, and sauté for 7–8 minutes until lightly golden. Add the bacon and chestnuts just before the end to heat through.

This purée plays on the deliciously aromatic flavor of Brussels sprouts, and with a bit of luck even those who normally decline could be tempted, not least because they probably won't recognise what it is unless you tell them.

brussels sprout and parsley purée

2 pounds Brussels sprouts, base
    trimmed and outer leaves discarded
2 scant teaspoons red wine vinegar
1¼ cups sour cream
4 tablespoons coarsely chopped
    fresh flat-leaf parsley
sea salt, black pepper
a dollop of salted butter

Serves 6

Bring a large pot of salted water to a boil, add the sprouts, and simmer for 15–20 minutes, until very tender. Drain them in a colander and leave for a minute or two to steam dry. Place them in the bowl of a food processor with the vinegar, sour cream, parsley, and some seasoning and blend to a smooth purée. Return the purée to the pot and gently reheat when required. Drop a dollop of butter into the center and serve.

If you know you have a house full of sprout-haters, and even a buttery purée is unlikely to pass muster, this is a fine alternative. It's great with any roast or pie. You could add some bits of chestnut too, and the bacon is optional.

green bean medley with crispy bacon

½ cup white wine

3 shallots, peeled and finely chopped

5 tablespoons unsalted butter, diced

14 ounces fine green beans, stalk ends trimmed

14 ounces sugar snaps, stalk ends trimmed

6 ounces bacon, diced

Serves 6

To make the sauce, place the wine and shallots in a small saucepan, bring to a boil and reduce to a couple of tablespoons, then whisk in the butter.

At the same time, bring a large pot of salted water to a boil. Cook the beans for 4–5 minutes, adding the sugar snaps 1 minute before the end, then drain them into a colander.

Meanwhile put the bacon into a large frying pan over medium heat, and fry in the rendered fat for 7–9 minutes until golden and crisp, stirring frequently. Drain on paper towel.

Toss the vegetables with the sauce, and mix in the bacon. You can also cook everything in advance, reheat the vegetables in the sauce, then add the bacon.

Savory lentils are delicious with roast ham. I also always dish them up with thick slices of bacon that we grill over an open fire. If you add a little more stock, and any tasty ends of ham or turkey, you have the makings of a hearty soup. The recipe is a basic—add any veggies you have on hand.

creamy lentils

2 tablespoons unsalted butter

2 slim carrots, peeled and thinly sliced

3 sticks of celery heart, trimmed
   and thinly sliced

5 garlic cloves, peeled and
   halved lengthways

1½ cups green lentils

1 quart vegetable or chicken stock

a pinch of dried chile flakes

1 bay leaf

sea salt

coarsely chopped fresh flat-leaf parsley
   to serve (optional)

Serves 6

Melt the butter in a medium-size saucepan over medium heat. Add the carrots and celery and fry for 6–7 minutes until softened and starting to color, stirring occasionally, adding the garlic shortly before the end. Add the lentils and cook for a minute or two longer, stirring, then add the stock, chile, and bay leaf. Bring to a boil, cover, and simmer for 25–40 minutes, until tender.

Discarding the bay leaf, put a few ladles of the lentils containing plenty of juices into a food processor and blend. Stir this back into the lentils, and season with salt. This part isn't essential, however. The lentils should be quite soupy at this point, so add a little more stock if necessary. You can also reheat them, in which case again you might need to add a little more stock. Serve scattered with parsley on top.

If you can't face juggling three different veggies, then this is the one for you—potatoes, parsnips, and sprouts roasted as one. A little honey drizzled over towards the end ensures the veggies arrive on the plate particularly sticky and caramelized.

all-in-one roasted veggies

2 pounds potatoes, peeled and cut
   into 1½-inch pieces
1¼ pounds parsnips, trimmed
   and peeled, halved, or quartered
   lengthways where thick and cut into
   2 shorter lengths
7 tablespoons unsalted butter, melted
sea salt, black pepper
1¼ pounds Brussels sprouts, base
   trimmed and outer leaves discarded
2 tablespoons honey

Serves 6

Preheat the oven to 400°F. Bring two medium pots of salted water to a boil. Add the potatoes to one and the parsnips to the other and cook for 5 minutes. Drain them into different sieves, and set aside for a few minutes for the surface moisture to evaporate. Return the potatoes to the pot and give them a shake, add a third of the butter and some seasoning and toss to coat them, then transfer them into a large roasting dish and cook for 10 minutes. Toss the parsnips with another third of the butter and some seasoning, then add to the potatoes in the roasting dish and cook for a further 45 minutes.

In the meantime, bring a medium-size pot of salted water to a boil. Add the sprouts and cook for 8 minutes, then drain them into a sieve and leave for a few minutes. Toss in the pan with the remaining butter and some seasoning.

Turn the temperature up to 425°F (i.e. on removing the turkey from the oven), mix the sprouts into the potatoes and parsnips, drizzle the honey on top, and cook for another 15–20 minutes until golden and caramelized.

The honey-mustard glaze here ensures that these bacon rolls emerge from the oven gorgeously sticky and golden. They also go down very well as cocktail nibbles if you are hunting for popular ideas, in which case make them small, using cocktail sausages.

honey-mustard sausage rolls

12 fresh pork sausages (12–14 ounces total)

peanut or vegetable oil (optional)

12 strips of bacon

1 tablespoon honey

1 tablespoon Dijon mustard

Serves 6–12

Preheat the oven to 400°F. Heat a large non-stick frying pan over medium-high heat and color the sausages all over for 5–7 minutes, adding a drop of oil to the pan if necessary. Wind a strip of bacon along the length of each sausage—you may like to secure them with a cocktail stick. Arrange the rolls, spaced slightly apart, in a roasting dish and roast for 20 minutes. In the meantime, blend the honey and mustard in a small bowl. Generously brush the sausages with the honey-mustard glaze on both sides and cook for another 15 minutes, until golden and sticky.

I prefer to slip out the insides of some good sausages rather than use sausage meat, as they are always that much better flavored.

sage, chestnut, and apple sausage meatballs

2 tablespoons unsalted butter

1 onion, peeled and finely chopped

1 apple, peeled, cored and
　finely diced

2 tablespoons fresh sage leaves,
　finely sliced

5½ ounces cooked and peeled
　chestnuts, sliced

sea salt, black pepper

1½ pounds sausages

Serves 6

Melt the butter in a large frying pan over medium heat, add the onion, apple, and sage, and fry for 5–6 minutes, until softened and glossy, without coloring. Add the chestnuts, season, and cook for a minute or two longer, then leave to cool.

Slit the sausages open and slip the meat into a large bowl. Add the chestnut mixture and combine. Take heaping tablespoons of the mixture and shape into balls. Cover and chill until required.

Preheat the oven to 350°F. Arrange the meatballs spaced a little way apart in a roasting dish and bake for 20 minutes. Turn the oven up to 425°F (i.e. on removing the turkey from the oven) and cook the meatballs for another 25 minutes or until they are golden.

In Europe, the ultimate stuffings are made with foie gras, and this little luxury that we can eat with a clear conscience is not dissimilar. It's also the cheat of the equation, a ten-minute dish if that. Any pâté can be used; my first choice would be either a pâté embellished with little morsels of mushroom, or a smooth pâté laced with apple. But there are any number of gorgeous Christmas options around.

faux foie gras stuffing

14 ounces pâté, diced

finely grated zest of 1 lemon

4 tablespoons coarsely chopped
   fresh flat-leaf parsley

1 tablespoon Madeira or Marsala

1¾ cups fresh white breadcrumbs

2 tablespoons unsalted butter

Serves 6
Makes enough stuffing
for an 11-pound turkey

Combine the pâté, lemon zest, parsley, Madeira or Marsala, and half the breadcrumbs in a bowl and stuff the turkey.

Up to an hour before eating, melt the butter in a large frying pan over medium heat. Once it is sizzling nicely, fry the remaining breadcrumbs until golden, stirring constantly, then transfer them to a bowl.

Spoon the stuffing out of the bird after carving, and serve with the breadcrumbs scattered on top.

A classic sage and onion stuffing has to be one of my favorite ways of filling the bird, and takes me back to Christmas Eve in my mother's kitchen, when she mixed it up in a large mixing bowl, covered it with a kitchen towel and it wafted the gentle scent of sage all afternoon and evening. It soaks up all the turkey juices from within as it cooks, and it's simple.

sage and onion stuffing

3½ tablespoons unsalted butter

2 large onions, peeled, quartered, and thinly sliced

1 tablespoon finely sliced fresh sage leaves

finely grated zest of 1 lemon, plus a squeeze of lemon juice

1¾ cups fresh white breadcrumbs

sea salt, black pepper

Serves 6
Makes enough stuffing for an 11-pound turkey

Melt half the butter in a large frying pan over medium heat, add the onions, and cook gently for 10–15 minutes, until lightly golden and caramelized, stirring frequently. Stir in the sage just before the end, then remove from the heat and add the lemon zest, a generous squeeze of lemon juice, and the remaining butter. Once this has melted add the breadcrumbs and season with salt and pepper.

in or out of the bird

The notion that stuffing the turkey is in some way dangerous is one of those myths. Provided you observe a few guidelines it is perfectly safe. That said, I always cook sausage meatballs outside the bird, but only because that caramelized golden exterior is too good to pass up, and "sausage balls" (for want of a more poetic description) are tantalizingly delicious.

Fill the main cavity of the turkey with the stuffing, packing it loosely, and leaving half the cavity empty but plugging the opening. This will allow the air to circulate inside the bird, in effect creating a mini oven. You can also stuff the neck end, using a different stuffing if you like or half an onion with a couple of sprigs of thyme or rosemary and a piece of lemon zest.

This lovely torte was born of a determination that there had to be a better way with nut roasts. So here we have the luxury of toasted almonds and cashews, with the succulence of spinach and molten goat cheese, in a recipe that doubles as a vegetarian main course or elegant stuffing cooked alongside the bird. What more could you ask?

homage to nut roast

2 pounds spinach

1¼ cups almond flakes

1 cup roasted cashews, chopped

finely grated zest of 1 lemon

2 teaspoons fresh thyme

sea salt, black pepper

3 tablespoons extra virgin olive oil
   or melted unsalted butter

4 tablespoons fresh white breadcrumbs

7 ounces medium-mature goat cheese,
   rind discarded, sliced

Serves 6–8

Bring a large pot of salted water to a boil, add the spinach, bring back to a boil, and cook for 2 minutes, then drain into a colander and leave to cool.

At the same time preheat the oven to 400°F, spread the almonds in a thin layer in a roasting dish or baking tray, and toast for 9–10 minutes until lightly golden.

Press out as much water as you can from the spinach using your hands, then slice or chop it. Place it in a large bowl, add the chopped cashews, flaked almonds, lemon zest, thyme, some seasoning, and a couple of tablespoons of olive oil or butter, and combine.

Toss the breadcrumbs with the remaining tablespoon of oil or butter and scatter half of them over the base of an 8-inch cake pan at least 1½ inches deep with a removable base. Press half the spinach mixture on top, then a layer of goat cheese and repeat with the remaining spinach. Scatter the rest of the breadcrumbs on top. You can prepare the torte to this point in advance, in which case cover and chill it.

Preheat the oven to 400°F and cook the torte for 35–40 minutes, until golden and crisp on the surface. Serve cut in wedges.

Turkey is unimaginable without this sweet and sour condiment. Just one tip: cooking the cranberries before adding the sugar avoids tough skins. That said, I don't think it's improved by the addition of spices or more alcohol—keep it simple.

cranberry sauce

1 pound cranberries
juice of 2 oranges
⅔ cup superfine sugar

Serves 6

Place the cranberries and orange juice in a small saucepan, bring to a boil, cover, and simmer over a low heat for 5 minutes. Stir in the sugar, turn the heat to medium, and simmer uncovered for another 10–15 minutes, until the juices are reduced and syrupy. Transfer the sauce to a bowl, cover with plastic wrap, and leave to cool.

This sauce can be prepared several days in advance, in which case chill and bring it back to room temperature before serving.

That sweet savor of onion and the hint of bay and cloves are what a bread sauce is all about, hence this version, which is a departure from the norm. Basically you make a creamy onion purée and combine it with a bread sauce base. It has the advantage that you can make it an hour or two ahead and then very gently rewarm it. I can't be alone in having a penchant for cold turkey and bread sauce sandwiches, so this is another one to cook plenty of, bearing in mind the days to come.

bread sauce

2 tablespoons unsalted butter
1 large onion (ideally white), peeled, halved, and sliced
¾ teaspoon sea salt
½ cup heavy cream
1 bay leaf
5 cloves
1¼ cups fresh white breadcrumbs
1 cup whole milk
freshly grated nutmeg

Serves 6

Melt the butter in a small non-stick saucepan over medium heat. Add the onion, sprinkle the salt on top, and cook gently for 6–8 minutes, stirring frequently, until soft and silky but not colored. Add the cream, bay leaf, and cloves, cover, and cook over the lowest heat for about 5 minutes, stirring at least once. Remove from the heat and leave to infuse for 20 minutes. Discard the bay leaf and cloves and blend to a smooth purée in a food processor.

Combine the breadcrumbs and milk in the same non-stick saucepan, and bring to a boil, stirring until smooth. Simmer for 7–10 minutes over low heat, stirring occasionally, until you have a thick sauce. Add the onion purée and heat through, and season with freshly grated nutmeg and a little more salt if needed. Unlike a normal bread sauce, this can be made in advance, anything up to a couple of hours. Cover the surface with plastic wrap and leave in the pan on the stove. Gently reheat to serve.

making breadcrumbs

Remove the crusts from some day-old coarse-textured white bread, break it up into chunks and blend in a food processor until reduced to fine crumbs. Should you have forgotten to buy the bread a day ahead you can use fresh bread, provided it is a good-quality rustic bread with a sturdy, dry crumb.

This is my basic gravy to go with the turkey. It make about 2 cups, but if you want even more, simply step up the ingredients accordingly, or you could make the extra gravy below.

gorgeous gravy

½ cup port
1 tablespoon all-purpose flour
2 cups giblet stock (see page 104)
   or chicken stock
sea salt, black pepper

Serves 6–8

Skim off any excess fat from the roasting pan leaving just 1 or 2 tablespoons. Place the roasting pan on a lowish heat, add the port, and cook for several minutes until reduced by half, scraping up all the sticky roasting juices in the bottom of the pan. Stir in the flour and once this is simmering, gradually stir in the stock. Simmer the gravy long and hard enough for it to amalgamate into a smooth sauce. Taste and season if necessary. Add any juices given out on carving the turkey and pour into a gravy boat to serve. If there are a lot of bits you might like to strain it first.

This is for whenever you want MORE gravy, without recourse to artificial powders. You could add a little Madeira or medium sherry in lieu of red wine for an even richer flavor.

extra gravy

2 tablespoons vegetable oil
2 pounds mixture of diced
   onion, celery, carrot, and leek
2 garlic cloves, peeled and
   finely chopped
1 tablespoon all-purpose flour
½ cup red wine
2 cups giblet stock (see page 104)
   or chicken stock
sea salt, black pepper

Serves 6–8

Heat the oil in a large pot over medium heat, then add the vegetables and fry for 30–35 minutes, stirring occasionally, until really well colored, almost black (this is your gravy browning). Add the garlic a few minutes before the end. Sprinkle the flour on top and stir, and then gradually add the red wine and cook for a couple of minutes, when it will thicken. Stir in the stock in two or three turns, add some seasoning, and simmer for about 5 minutes. Pass the gravy through a sieve, pressing out as much as possible from the vegetables. If it tastes at all thin, you can simmer it a few minutes longer, and check the seasoning. If you let it stand for any length of time, then there may be a little oil on the surface, which you can skim off. Add any juices given out on slicing the roast.

A rich, creamy gravy that makes a luxurious touch with Christmas dinner. The sweet wine can be varied; skim off a little of whatever you have bought in to drink.

sauternes gravy

½ teaspoon Dijon mustard
½ cup Sauternes or sweet wine
1 tablespoon all-purpose flour
1 cup giblet or chicken stock
½ cup heavy cream
sea salt, black pepper

Serves 6–8

Skim off any excess fat from the roasting pan, leaving just 1 or 2 tablespoons. Place the roasting pan on a lowish heat, stir in the mustard, then the Sauternes, and cook for several minutes until reduced by half, scraping up all the sticky roasting juices in the bottom of the pan. Stir in the flour and once this is simmering, gradually stir in the stock and the cream. Simmer the gravy until you have a smooth sauce, and season to taste—the Sauternes welcomes a generous pinch or two of salt. Add any juices given out on carving the turkey and strain into a gravy boat to serve.

giblet stock

turkey or goose gizzard, neck bone,
    and heart
1 tablespoon goose fat or peanut oil
sea salt, black pepper
2 cups water or chicken stock

Serves 6–8
Makes approx. 2 cups

Preheat the oven to 425°F. If buying your bird from a friendly butcher, you could prevail upon them to chop up the gizzard and neck bone for you. Otherwise, chop the heart and place it together with the whole gizzard and neck bone in a small roasting dish. Drizzle with a tablespoon of goose fat or peanut oil, season with salt and pepper, and roast for 20 minutes until lightly colored. Place the giblets in a small saucepan with the water or chicken stock, (keeping hold of the roasting dish if you're making gravy for the roast goose with prune and apple stuffing on page 54). Bring to a simmer, skim the surface if necessary, cover, and simmer over a very low heat for 30–45 minutes, then strain.

lovely leftovers

Where do we begin? In England, Boxing Day, the day after Christmas, brings with it a culture of eating all on its own, that's as ad hoc as a game of charades. When hunger strikes it's each to their own whim, my own being those heartstoppingly good bread sauce and turkey sandwiches. When no one's looking, that is, just as few would care to admit to mulled wine trifle for breakfast, and other such outlandish snacking.

Writ large in all the cooking we do for Christmas is providing the leftovers that will feed us in their own sweet tradition in the days between Christmas and New Year. Turkey should always be ordered a size larger than you are likely to want on the day for the dividend thereafter, all that succulent dark meat that clings to the bones but evaded carving, and the gorgeous brown stock that results from the carcass. No other potful matches it at any other stage of the year. It is the foundation for soups galore, and for the must-eat turkey and ham pie. Which leads us to the other great roast to enjoy in excess, ham. Its poaching liquor, providing the ham is unsmoked, makes for fabulous lentil soups, and any leftover morsel will be lauded in all manner of salads, pies, and grilled sandwiches.

Cold leftover veggies make a fine frying-pan hash, nicely peppered up with chile. Even the leftover stuffing can be put to good use, with some salad leaves and a lightly poached egg, as a kind of inside-out Scotch egg. While leftover Christmas pudding or cake will lend themselves to a divine bread-and-butter-style dessert in lieu of the panettone on page 137.

Sweet, thick, and mealy, and full of the scent of Christmas. You want a good old-fashioned sausage here for the crispy bits though beware of wandering fingers if they're sitting around for any length of time.

chestnut and madeira soup with crispy sausage

3½ tablespoons unsalted butter

1 onion, peeled and chopped

1 celery heart, trimmed and sliced

2 carrots, trimmed, peeled, and sliced

1 parsnip, trimmed, peeled, and sliced

1 pound cooked and peeled chestnuts

½ cup Madeira

5 cups turkey or other poultry stock

sea salt, black pepper

1 tablespoon peanut or vegetable oil

3 sausages (approx. ½ pound), skinned

coarsely chopped fresh flat-leaf parsley to serve

Serves 6

Melt the butter in a large pot over medium heat, add the onion, celery, carrots, and parsnip, and fry for about 10 minutes, stirring frequently, until softened and lightly golden. Add the chestnuts and cook for a minute or two longer, then add the Madeira and simmer until well reduced. Pour in the stock, add some seasoning, bring to a boil, and simmer for 15 minutes, until the vegetables are tender. Purée the soup in a blender, then return it to the pot, and taste for seasoning.

Heat the oil in a large non-stick frying pan over medium heat. Roughly slice and add the sausage meat, and cook for 6–9 minutes until golden and caramelized, breaking it up into little pieces with a metal spatula as it gets firm, so you end up with lots of little crispy bits. Drain it on a double layer of paper towels. Serve the hot soup with some of the crispy sausage in the center, and some chopped parsley on top.

If you're thinking about this for the main course, then I would make two or three times the amount of Stilton toasts, as they disappear with or without the soup. In fact they make very good cocktail nibbles too.

celeriac and apple soup

Soup

5 tablespoons unsalted
  butter
2 onions, peeled and
  chopped
2 leeks, trimmed and sliced
2 carrots, trimmed, peeled
  and diced
1 celery heart, trimmed
  and sliced
1 celeriac bulb (2 pounds),
  peeled and diced

1 apple, peeled, cored,
  and diced
1 cup dry cider
5 cups turkey or other
  poultry or vegetable stock
sea salt, black pepper

Toasts

6 thin slices of baguette
unsalted butter
2½ ounces Stilton, crumbled

Serves 6

Melt the butter in a large pot over medium-low heat. Add the onions, leeks, carrots, and celery and cook gently for 10–12 minutes, until glossy and starting to color, stirring occasionally. Add the celeriac and apple and cook for about 5 minutes longer. Pour in the cider and cook until well reduced, then add the stock and some seasoning, bring to a boil, and simmer for 20 minutes, until the celeriac is tender. Purée the soup in a blender in batches and press it through a sieve, then adjust the seasoning.

To make the Stilton toasts, heat the broiler and toast the baguette slices on both sides. Spread with butter, crumble the Stilton on top, and return to the broiler until melted and sizzling. Reheat the soup if necessary, ladle into bowls and float the toasts in the soup.

Buy in lots of these root vegetables before Christmas; they'll keep well in the veggie bin and make for a fabulously aromatic thick sweet soup that's given a savory edge by a rich turkey stock.

parsnip and rosemary soup

Soup

3½ tablespoons unsalted butter

2 onions, peeled and chopped

1 leek, trimmed and sliced

4 sticks of celery heart, trimmed
  and sliced

2 garlic cloves, peeled and finely chopped

1¼ pounds parsnips, trimmed, peeled,
  halved, and sliced

4 x 4-inch sprigs of fresh rosemary

juice of ½ lemon

4 cups turkey or other poultry
  or vegetable stock

sea salt, black pepper

½ cup heavy or whipping cream

Bits

9 ounces bacon, diced

⅓ cup pine nuts

Serves 6

Melt the butter in a large pot over medium-low heat. Add the onions, leek, celery, and garlic and cook gently for 15–20 minutes, until softened and glossy, stirring occasionally. Add the parsnips, rosemary, and lemon juice and cook for another 15 minutes, again stirring occasionally. Add the stock and some seasoning, bring to a boil, and simmer for 10 minutes. Remove the rosemary sprigs and blend the soup; you may need to do this in batches. Stir in the cream and taste for seasoning.

Shortly before serving, put the bacon in a large frying pan over medium heat and fry until golden and crisp, stirring frequently. Transfer it to a double layer of paper towels to drain. Now cook the pine nuts in the bacon fat until golden, stirring almost constantly, and drain these on paper towels as well. Once cool, combine the bacon and nuts in a bowl and serve scattered on top of the hot soup.

Butternut squash and scallops go together wonderfully, but the soup will be just as good on its own, or with a little Stilton, or some bits of ham. The stock is all-important here, and needs to be a little bit stronger than usual.

butternut squash soup with saffron cream

Soup

3½ tablespoons unsalted
  butter
1 large onion, peeled
  and chopped
1 celery heart, trimmed
  and sliced
2 leeks, trimmed and sliced
3 garlic cloves, peeled and
  finely chopped
4½ pounds butternut squash,
  skin and seeds removed,
  cut into chunks
3–3½ cups strong turkey or
  other poultry stock
sea salt, white pepper
juice of ½ lemon

Saffron Cream

approx. 20 saffron filaments,
  ground and blended with
  1 teaspoon boiling water
1 cup sour cream

Scallops

12 plump scallops
1 tablespoon extra virgin
  olive oil
a squeeze of lemon juice
coarsely chopped fresh
  flat-leaf parsley

Serves 6

Melt the butter in a large pot over medium heat. Add the onion, celery, and leeks and cook gently for about 10 minutes, until glossy, softened, and just starting to color. Stir occasionally and add the garlic shortly before the end. Add the squash and cook for a few minutes longer, stirring often, then add the stock and press the vegetables down— they may not be completely covered. Season with plenty of salt and a little pepper, bring to a boil, cover, and simmer for 15 minutes. Purée the soup in batches in a blender, then stir in the lemon juice and taste for seasoning. You should have a thick, silky orange soup.

Blend the saffron infusion with the sour cream and a little salt in a bowl. To prepare the scallops, pull the corals away from the white meat, removing the surrounding girdle and the white gristle at the same time. Cut off and reserve the corals and slice the meat into discs. Toss these in a bowl with the olive oil and some seasoning. Heat a large non-stick frying pan over high heat, and briefly sear about a third of the scallops at a time until lightly caramelized, about 30 seconds each side. Once they are all cooked squeeze a little lemon juice on top. Serve the hot soup with a little of the saffron cream, some of the scallops, and a sprinkling of parsley on top.

Something warming and spicy for the post-Christmas chill, usually made with chicken, but turkey does just as nicely. Don't be put off by the lengthy list of ingredients—its charm is its complexity and it's comparatively quick to make.

turkey mulligatawny

2 tablespoons unsalted butter

2 leeks, trimmed and thinly sliced

2 sticks of celery, trimmed
  and thinly sliced

2 medium carrots or 1 large,
  trimmed, peeled, halved, and sliced

2 teaspoons finely grated fresh ginger

1 medium-hot fresh red chile,
  de-seeded and finely diced

1 teaspoon turmeric

½ teaspoon ground cumin

½ teaspoon ground coriander

½ pound potatoes, peeled and cut
  into ½-inch dice

1 bay leaf

5 cups turkey stock

sea salt

¼ cup basmati rice

¾ cup coconut milk

5½ ounces cooked turkey, cut into
  fine strips

2 tablespoons lemon juice

coarsely chopped fresh cilantro
  to serve

Serves 6

Melt the butter in a large pot over medium heat, add the leeks, celery, carrots, ginger, and chile and fry for about 5 minutes until softened, stirring frequently. Stir in the spices and then the potatoes, and add the bay leaf. Pour in the stock and season with salt, then bring to a boil, and simmer over low heat for 10 minutes. Stir in the rice and cook for another 10–15 minutes, until it is tender.

At the end of cooking, add the coconut milk, the turkey, and the lemon juice and taste for seasoning. Reheat the soup almost to boiling point. You can either serve the mulligatawny as it is, or briefly blend it in a food processor to a thick textured soup, first removing the bay leaf. Serve in warm bowls, scattered with cilantro.

For those who find Stilton a little too assertive, I would opt for a big wedge of Wensleydale on the sideboard. It's a really elegant cheese, sharp and buttery and just the ticket with after-dinner dates.

chicory, wensleydale, hazelnut, and date salad

Salad

⅓ cup peeled hazelnuts
4 heads of chicory, base trimmed
handful of Bibb or Boston lettuce
6 medjool dates, quartered lengthways
5½ ounces Wensleydale or Stilton, cut
   into ½-inch dice

Dressing

1 tablespoon red wine vinegar
1 teaspoon Dijon mustard
½ teaspoon superfine sugar
sea salt, black pepper
4 tablespoons hazelnut oil
4 tablespoons peanut oil

Serves 6

Preheat the oven to 400°F. Scatter the nuts over the base of a small cookie sheet and toast for 9–10 minutes, until golden. Leave to cool, then halve or coarsely chop them.

To make the dressing, whisk the vinegar with a tablespoon of water, the mustard, sugar, and some seasoning, then whisk in the oils until amalgamated. Discarding the outer chicory leaves if they are damaged, finely slice the heads lengthways. Combine the leaves, dates, and hazelnuts in a large salad bowl. The salad can be prepared to this point up to an hour in advance, in which case cover and set aside in a cool place.

To serve, give the dressing a whisk, pour on top of the salad, and toss, then gently mix in the cheese.

Chantenay carrots are small and plump with a lovely flavor and texture. There is no need to peel them, and they look particularly good in a salad. This one's great with sliced roast ham.

roasted carrot and parsnip salad with crunchy seeds

2 tablespoons sunflower seeds

2 tablespoons pumpkin seeds

1 tablespoon sesame seeds

5 tablespoons extra virgin olive oil

1 pound Chantenay or baby organic carrots

sea salt, black pepper

1 pound parsnips, trimmed, peeled, and cut into batons

2 tablespoons white wine vinegar

1 teaspoon honey

½ cup fresh smooth orange juice

handful arugula or Bibb lettuce

Serves 6–8

Preheat the oven to 400°F. Scatter the seeds over the base of a cookie sheet and toast for 9–10 minutes, then leave to cool.

Heat a tablespoon of oil in a large frying pan over high heat. Add the carrots and some seasoning and fry for 4–8 minutes, stirring occasionally, until colored. Put them into a roasting dish, and color the parsnips in the same way, adding another tablespoon of oil to the pan (these will color a little quicker). Blend the vinegar with the honey in a bowl, stir in the orange juice, and then pour on top of the carrots and parsnips. Roast for 25 minutes, by which time the liquid should have evaporated and the vegetables be tender. Drizzle with another 3 tablespoons of oil and scatter more sea salt on top. Leave to cool.

Sprinkle the seeds over the veggies, then gently mix in the salad leaves and transfer to a serving bowl.

So just what do you do with all that leftover stuffing? It was after eating a Scotch egg at the French-inspired restaurant La Trompette in Chiswick, West London, that I dreamed up this deconstructed version in the hope of revisiting it. Theirs was a soft runny yolk within a sausage meat casing that spilled as you cut into it. This cannot claim any such technical greatness, but is a friendly plate of grub all the same.

inside-out scotch egg

approx. 2 cups stuffing (ideally a
    sausage one)
a mixture of arugula leaves, sprigs
    of fresh cilantro, dill, and parsley,
    to serve 4
white wine vinegar
4 large eggs, preferably organic
peanut oil
lemon juice
sea salt

Serves 4

Fill your largest pot with water and bring it to a boil. Arrange the stuffing on four large plates. Place the salad leaves in a large bowl. Add a good slug of white wine vinegar to the boiling water. Now turn the heat down and keep the water at a trembling simmer while the eggs are poaching.

Break the eggs one at a time into a teacup (or use four teacups). Gently stir the water into a whirlpool using a large spoon and drop the eggs into it. They will immediately sink to the bottom of the pot, leaving strands of white floating. After about 4 minutes, remove them using a slotted spoon, trimming off the tendrils of white against the side of the pot.

Place the poached eggs on top of the stuffing. Toss the leaves with just enough oil to coat them, a few drops of lemon juice, and a pinch of sea salt and divide between the plates. Serve immediately.

A big plate of hash peppered with Lea & Perrins is essential to the post-Christmas proceedings, and you can include any leftover veggies as well as cooking them from scratch as suggested. A large frying pan will do for two to three, so if you are more than this, double the quantities and use two pans.

ham and root veggie hash

½ pound carrots, trimmed,
    peeled, and diced
½ pound rutabaga, peeled and diced
½ pound parsnips, trimmed,
    peeled, and diced
3 tablespoons extra virgin olive oil
1 red onion, peeled, halved, and sliced
2 sprigs of fresh rosemary
3 medium-hot red chiles
4 garlic cloves, peeled
sea salt
3 slices of roast ham, cut into
    broad strips

Serves 2–3

Place the carrots, rutabaga, and parsnips in the top half of a steamer placed over about an inch of simmering water in the lower half and steam for 15 minutes. At the same time heat the olive oil in a large frying pan over medium-low heat and gently cook the onion for 12–15 minutes, stirring frequently, until nicely golden and slightly crisp. Transfer to a bowl and reserve.

Add the steamed vegetables to the frying pan with the rosemary, chiles, and garlic cloves and sauté, again over medium-low heat, for about 25 minutes, turning them frequently. Season with salt halfway through. At the end of cooking add the onions and ham to heat through. Discard the rosemary and garlic cloves and serve. The flesh of the chiles can be eaten, scraped off the skin.

This Coronation turkey makes a lovely sandwich or serve it with a rice salad, scattering some toasted almond flakes, pine nuts, and some chopped cilantro on top. Don't be put off by the long list of ingredients, it's all said and done in 30 minutes. You could also use chicken.

coronation turkey with apricots

2 tomatoes
⅓ teaspoon ground cumin
⅓ teaspoon ground coriander
¼ teaspoon turmeric
⅛ teaspoon cayenne pepper
¼ teaspoon ground cinnamon
¼ teaspoon ground ginger
1 cup peanut oil, plus
    2 tablespoons
1 onion, peeled, halved, and
    thinly sliced
½ cup dried apricots, boiled in
    water for 10 minutes, sliced
sea salt
1 medium egg yolk
1 teaspoon Dijon mustard
a squeeze of lemon juice
black pepper
1 pound cooked turkey meat,
    cut into strips
mustard greens to serve

Serves 4

Bring a small pot of water to a boil. Cut out a cone from the top of each tomato, dunk them into the boiling water for 20 seconds and then into cold water. Remove them, slip off the skins, and coarsely chop them. Combine all the spices in a bowl.

Heat the 2 tablespoons of oil in a large frying pan over medium-low heat, add the onion, and sauté for several minutes, until soft and translucent. Add the spices and give them a stir, then add the tomatoes and apricots and season with salt. Turn the heat down low and cook for 8–12 minutes, until the sauce is thick and reduced and the oil separates from the tomatoes, stirring frequently. Transfer the mixture to a bowl or plate and leave to cool.

Whisk the egg yolk with the mustard in a bowl, then slowly whisk in the cup of peanut oil, just a few drops at a time to begin with. Combine the mayonnaise with the cooled tomato and onion mixture, add a squeeze of lemon juice, and a grinding of black pepper. Stir in the turkey, sprinkle the mustard and greens on top, and season to taste.

christmas desserts

You don't even have to like Christmas pudding to be filled with contented pleasure at that moment after a big Christmas dinner, when the lights are turned out and the Christmas pudding lit with a halo of blue flame is ceremoniously carried in. It is one of the great rituals of the festivities in England. And most of us manage just a small spoonful of this incredibly rich dessert. A succulent mass of dried fruits and spices, fused with molten suet (if you can find it), and infused with brandy, every time I make one I find it a matter of wonder that this loose mixture can turn into the dark sophisticated dessert that it does simply with many hours of steaming.

My mother always used to serve it with a lily-white rum custard as well as brandy butter, which is every bit as delectable as bread sauce with turkey. This is the recipe I grew up with, and the only shortcut I have taken is with the suet, which my mother used to grate by hand. She always made it well in advance of Christmas, so it is one to get mixing on "Stir-up Sunday," four Sundays before Christmas, or at least in time for it to mature. Should you be looking for something lighter, with just a little in the way of dried fruit and booze to set the tone, then a panettone dessert is probably the one for you, a Christmassy bread and butter dessert.

Next on the list is something with chestnuts. The bûche de Noël on page 166 will stand in for a Christmas pudding, and the little mont blancs in a glass are heavenly eaten with meringues. I love a trifle on Boxing Day, the day after Christmas. It seems the perfect dessert to wheel out after the ham, soothing layer upon layer of jelly and sponge cake, custard, and syllabub, and this of course can be made a couple of days in advance, to its credit. While by contrast a wobbly red cranberry delight not only sings with goodness but makes an ethereal end to any rich meal. My family loves this white Christmas version of a cheesecake, as well as the chocolatey tiramisu torte.

my grandmother's christmas pudding

This is the Christmas pudding I grew up with; it's really dark, rich, and moist, a recipe my mother thinks she was given by my paternal grandmother. It's on a well-stained page in her handwritten book of recipes, in faded ink, with no instructions at all, simply a list of ingredients, but she's filled me in with the rest. She used to mature these puddings one year for the next, on the top shelf of a cupboard in my bedroom, and the lingering scent that escaped every time it was opened lies deep in my memory. To be on the safe side, though, if maturing it for a year I prefer the fridge.

Traditionally it should be made on "Stir-up Sunday," the weekend before Advent, four Sundays before Christmas. The "stir-up" actually has nothing to do with making the pudding itself; rather it is taken from the collect for the day in the Church of England's Book of Common Prayer, read after the communion:

"Stir-up, we beseech thee, O Lord, the wills of thy faithful people;
That they, plenteously bringing forth the fruit of good works, may of thee
be plenteously rewarded; through Jesus Christ our Lord."

So returning from church to your kitchen, ravenous, you take it in turns with the rest of the family to give the pudding mixture a stir, east to west in honor of the Three Wise Men, and to make a silent wish. You include a coin at your own risk, you could also include a ring, as a symbol of marriage, and a thimble brings good luck.

½ pound seedless raisins

¼ pound golden raisins

1 glass of brandy (approx. ½ cup),
   plus extra to flambé

¼ pound demerara sugar

½ pound shredded beef suet (ask your
   butcher)

½ pound white breadcrumbs

⅓ cup ground rice flour

½ teaspoon ground ginger

½ teaspoon ground cinnamon

½ teaspoon ground nutmeg

½ teaspoon sea salt

2 apples, peeled, cored, and diced

⅓ cup chopped mixed peel

¼ cup chopped almonds

2 medium eggs, beaten

2 tablespoons whole milk

holly to decorate

Each pudding serves 6–8
Makes 2

Mix the dried fruits in a large mixing bowl and pour the brandy on top. Add all the remaining ingredients (except the holly), and take it in turns to stir the pudding from east to west while making your wish, taking care to mix it well. Butter two 6-inch pudding basins (see page 9) and place a square of parchment paper in the bottom of each one. Divide the mixture between them, pressing it down well—the pudding won't expand hugely, but there should be about ½ inch of room at the top. Cover with a sheet of parchment paper that comes about halfway down the sides, and tie it in place with string.

Cooking the puddings can be steamy stuff, and the best method is to either place them in one or two cast-iron pots with tightly fitting lids, or in one large pot, wrapping the lid in a clean kitchen towel so the corners drape over the top. Fill the pots with water to cover half the pudding basins, bring to a boil, add the puddings, cover, and steam for 6 hours, adding water every 2 hours or so as necessary. Leave to cool completely in the pots, then remove the paper, re-cover, and store in a cool dry place until Christmas.

On the day, steam for 2 hours as above to serve, then run a knife around the edge, place a plate on top, and invert the pudding to turn it out. Stick with a sprig of holly and flambé with brandy.

This lily-white custard is heavenly poured over Christmas pudding, which doesn't mean missing out on the brandy butter, have a little dab of that too. But it does need to be made to order and served immediately, so have everything at the ready and heat it just before eating. It's yummy served over hot mince pies (see page 150) as a dessert too.

rum sauce

2 cups whole milk
2 tablespoons cornstarch
½ cup heavy cream
2 tablespoons dark rum
½ cup superfine sugar

Serves 6–8

Blend a little of the milk with the cornstarch in a small bowl. Add this to a small non-stick saucepan with the rest of the ingredients, bring to a boil, stirring as it thickens, and serve immediately.

The secret here is to whisk the butter until it is really light and fluffy, almost white.

brandy butter

12 tablespoons unsalted butter, softened
1⅓ cups confectioners's sugar, sifted
5 tablespoons brandy or Armagnac

Serves 6–8

Whisk the butter in a bowl until it is really pale and mousse-like, using a hand blender. Add the sugar and whisk again. Gradually beat in the brandy or Armagnac until you have a smooth creamy butter. Transfer to a bowl, cover, and chill until required. Take the butter out of the fridge about 20 minutes before serving.

All the fun of the fair, these baked apples come bathed in a sparkling, rich caramel sauce. You could also jazz up the filling with a few spices, ground cinnamon, ginger, and cloves.

baked toffee apples

2 tablespoons unsalted butter, softened
3 tablespoons light brown sugar
finely grated zest of 1 lemon,
    plus 1 tablespoon juice
¼ cup raisins
2½ tablespoons currants
6 red apples
6 tablespoons corn syrup
1 tablespoon dark rum or water
whipped cream to serve

Serves 6

Preheat the oven to 350°F. Cream the butter and sugar together in a small bowl, then beat in the lemon zest and juice (don't worry if the mixture appears a little curdled at this point). Mix in the raisins and currants. Using the tip of a sharp knife, incise a circle around the middle of each apple. This ensures that as it cooks the apple has room to expand without the skin splitting. Now cut out the core. The easiest way to do this, unless you have an apple corer, is to remove a cone from the top and bottom of each one, and then trim the center. If you try and slip out the whole center from one end you can end up splitting the apple in two.

Loosely stuff the cavities with the dried fruit mixture to within ½ inch of the top, and place the apples in a baking dish spaced slightly apart. Drizzle a tablespoon of syrup on top of each one and bake for 45 minutes, basting them every 15 minutes. Place the apples on plates, or transfer them to a serving dish and leave to cool for 10–15 minutes. Pour the syrup into a small saucepan, spooning any loose raisins and currants back inside the apples. Simmer until reduced by half and a deep caramel gold color, then stir in a tablespoon of rum or water. Drizzle the caramel over the apples and serve with cream.

An old-fashioned trifle with sponge cakes soaked in orange syrup, spread with strawberry jam and a fluffy syllabub on top, run through with a heady hit of almonds courtesy of the amaretti and amaretto. So nothing lavish then.

almond trifle

Base

4 medium oranges

2½ tablespoons superfine sugar

6–10 ladyfingers or leftover sponge
  cake

1 cup strawberry jam

10 amaretti, plus a few more to serve

1½ tablespoons almond flakes

confectioners' sugar for dusting

Syllabub

finely grated zest of 1 orange,
  plus 2 tablespoons juice

a generous squeeze of lemon juice

½ cup sweet sherry

2 tablespoons amaretto

⅓ cup confectioners' sugar

1 cup heavy cream

Serves 8

Halve and juice two of the oranges, and put into a small saucepan with the superfine sugar over medium heat. Simmer until reduced to approx. 4 tablespoons of syrup. Arrange the ladyfingers on the base of an 8-inch trifle dish at least 3 inches deep, cutting them to fit and squeezing them in, and splash the syrup on top. Place the jam in a bowl and work it with a spoon until it is smooth, then spread it over the ladyfingers.

Slice the skin and outer pith off the remaining 2 oranges and run a small sharp knife between the segments to remove them from the pith that separates them. Drain the segments into a sieve placed over a bowl, then scatter them on top of the ladyfingers. Arrange the ten amaretti on top.

To make the syllabub, whisk the orange zest and juice with the lemon juice, sherry, amaretto, and confectioners' sugar in a large bowl. Slowly whisk in the cream in a thin stream, and continue to whisk until you have a light and fluffy syllabub. While it needs to be the consistency of softly whipped cream, care should be taken not to overwhisk, otherwise it can separate. I use a hand blender for this. Smooth the syllabub over the trifle base, cover with plastic wrap, and chill overnight. During this time the syllabub will firm, and the syrup and juices will continue to soak into the ladyfingers, which should be very moist by the time you serve it.

Scatter the almonds over the base of a baking dish and toast for 7–8 minutes in an oven preheated to 350°F.

Just before serving, arrange a few amaretti in the center, scatter most of the almond flakes on top, with a few around the edge, and dust with confectioners' sugar.

This trifle's a voyage of jelly and custard, with strains of spicy mulled wine, or muddled wine as my son would call it, and little jellied fruit slices that complete the punch bowl effect.

mulled wine trifle

Base

½ cup sweet white wine

3 tablespoons brandy

½ cup fresh smooth orange juice

6 cloves

2 star anise

1 cinnamon stick

¼ cup superfine sugar

¼ ounce of powdered gelatin,
   *(see page 147)

approx. 6–10 ladyfingers or
   leftover sponge cake

⅔ cup raspberry jam

Custard

4 medium egg yolks

⅔ cup confectioners' sugar, sifted

½ cup all-purpose flour, sifted

1½ cups whole milk

2 strips of orange peel, removed
   with a potato peeler

On Top

1 cup heavy cream

jellied orange and lemon slices

Serves 8

Bring the wine, brandy, orange juice, spices, and sugar to a boil in a small saucepan. Stir to dissolve the sugar, then leave to infuse for 5 minutes. In the meantime, place the gelatin in a bowl, cover with cold water, and leave to soak for 5 minutes, then drain. Pour some of the hot wine solution over the soaked gelatin, stir until it dissolves, then stir this back into the rest of the solution.

Arrange the ladyfingers over the base of an 8-inch trifle bowl 3–4 inches deep, cutting them to fit. Strain the wine solution on top, leave to cool, then cover and chill for several hours or until set.

In the meantime make the custard. Whisk the egg yolks and confectioners' sugar together in a medium-size non-stick saucepan until smooth, then whisk in the flour a third at a time, until you have a thick creamy paste. Bring the milk to a boil in a small saucepan with the orange peel, and whisk it into the egg mixture a little at a time, until it is all incorporated. Return the pan to a low heat and cook for a few minutes until the custard thickens, stirring vigorously with a wooden spoon to disperse any lumps that form; if necessary you can give it a quick whisk. The custard shouldn't actually boil, but the odd bubble will ensure that it's hot enough to thicken properly. Cook it for a few minutes longer, again stirring constantly. Discard the orange zest, pour the custard into a bowl, cover the surface with plastic wrap, and leave to cool.

To assemble the trifle, work the jam in a bowl to loosen it, then spread it over the surface of the ladyfingers and gelatin. Give the custard a stir with a spoon to smooth it, and spread this over the jam. Whisk the cream in a bowl until it forms soft peaks and spread it over the top of the custard. Cover and chill for a couple of hours or overnight. Decorate with jellied slices just before serving.

Panettone could have been created especially for bread and butter pudding—replete with dried fruit and candied peel, it turns an old favorite into a Christmas great. A nice plump loaf should still leave plenty for dessert.

pear and panettone pudding

3 medium eggs

¾ cup superfine sugar

1½ cups heavy cream

1½ cups whole milk

1 tablespoon dark rum (optional)

salted butter, softened

10–15 x ½-inch slices of panettone
   (cut as wedges from a
   1½ pound loaf)

2 slightly underripe pears, peeled,
   quartered, cored, and sliced
   lengthways

⅓ cup apricot jam, warmed
   and sieved (optional)

Serves 6

Preheat the oven to 350°F. Whisk the eggs and sugar in a bowl, then whisk in the cream, milk, and rum. Butter the panettone and arrange lengthways in overlapping slices to cover the base of a 14-inch oval gratin or other shallow ovenproof dish. The center may take two slices side by side, while the narrow ends will only hold one. Scatter the pears over the top. Pour the custard through a sieve over and around the panettone and fruit.

Place the gratin dish in a roasting dish with cold water that comes two-thirds of the way up the sides. Bake for 1 hour, until the custard is puffy and set and the bread golden. Brush the surface of the bread with the apricot jam (this bit is optional but it gives the pudding a lovely sticky glaze). Serve immediately.

This is one of those rich and glamorous chocolate creations that will either make a decadent afternoon treat or an elegant dessert. I can never resist the shimmer of gold and silver dragées and the like, and this is just the right place to show them off.

tiramisu torte

Cake

½ cup self-rising flour

½ cup light brown sugar

3½ tablespoons peanut oil

1 medium egg, separated

1 tablespoon espresso, or very strong
  black coffee, cooled

1 tablespoon whole milk

Filling

10½ ounces dark chocolate (approx.
  50% cocoa), broken into pieces

4 medium eggs, separated

2½ tablespoons superfine sugar

9 ounces mascarpone

2 tablespoons Kahlua or very
  strong black coffee

edible gold or silver decorations,
  e.g. sprinkles, dragées, chocolate
  stars or leaf

Serves 6–8

Preheat the oven to 375°F and butter an 8-inch cake pan at least 1½ inches deep with a removable base. Sift the flour and sugar into a medium bowl. Add the oil, egg yolk, espresso, and milk and beat with a wooden spoon until smooth. Whisk the egg white until stiff in another bowl, I use a hand blender for this, and fold into the mixture in two turns. Spoon this into the prepared pan, covering the base evenly, and give the pan a couple of sharp taps on the work surface to allow any bubbles to rise. Bake in the oven for 12–15 minutes until lightly golden, firm when pressed, and shrinking from the sides. Leave to cool.

Place the chocolate in a bowl placed over a pan with a little simmering water in it and gently melt. Remove the bowl from the heat and leave the chocolate to cool to room temperature if necessary. Whisk the egg whites until stiff in a largish bowl, then whisk the egg yolks and sugar in another bowl until very pale and mousse-like.

Add the mascarpone to the melted chocolate and blend, then fold in the egg yolk mixture, and then the egg whites in two batches. Stir in the Kahlua or coffee. Smooth the chocolate cream over the cake base, cover, and chill for several hours or overnight. Decorate with gold or silver decorations, run a knife around the collar, and remove it, serving the torte in slices.

An unctuously creamy white chocolate cheesecake that panders to our aspirations for a white Christmas. This would be delicious served with a little fruit compote, a cranberry one for dramatics.

white christmas cheesecake

Crust
3½ tablespoons unsalted butter
approx. 2½ cups Graham crackers, crushed

Filling
½ ounce powdered gelatin, (see page 147)
3⅓ cups sour cream
½ cup superfine sugar
1 teaspoon vanilla extract
3 ounces white chocolate, broken into pieces
1¾ cups ricotta
white chocolate shavings to decorate

Serves 6–8
Makes 1 x 8-inch cake

Gently melt the butter in a small saucepan over low heat. Place the Graham crackers inside a plastic bag and crush them to fine crumbs using a rolling pin. Pour them into the saucepan with the melted butter and stir to coat them, then transfer to an 8-inch cake pan 10 inches deep with a removable base. Using your fingers or the bottom of a tumbler, press them into the base, making sure you seal the edges, and place in the fridge while you do the next stage.

Place the gelatin in a bowl, cover with cold water, and soak for 5 minutes, then drain. Pour 3 tablespoons of boiling water over the soaked gelatin and stir to dissolve. Place the sour cream in a small saucepan with the sugar and gently heat, stirring constantly with a wooden spoon until the mixture liquefies and the sugar has dissolved. Give the mixture a quick whisk to get rid of any lumps. It should be warm, roughly the same temperature as the gelatin solution. Stir the gelatin into the sour cream mixture, along with the vanilla extract, then transfer to a bowl and leave to cool.

Gently melt the chocolate in a bowl placed over a pan with a little simmering water in it. Put the ricotta in the bowl of a food processor and blend until smooth, add the melted chocolate, and blend again, then add the cream and sugar mixture and bend once more. Pour this mixture on top of the cheesecake base. Cover with plastic wrap and chill overnight. Decorate with chocolate shavings before serving.

An instant, luxurious, and hedonistic affair in the company of whipped cream (or Chantilly, to give it a lacy name), and meringues—most good pâtisseries sell big cloud-like oversized ones that make for glamorous rustic eating.

mont blanc in a glass

15½ ounces of unsweetened
   chestnut purée
4 tablespoons corn syrup
2 tablespoons dark rum
1 cup heavy cream
cocoa for dusting
meringues to serve

Serves 6

Blend the chestnut purée, syrup, and rum in a food processor until smooth. Divide between six ½-cup glasses, mounding it with a tablespoon. Whisk the cream to firm peaks in a bowl, I use a hand blender, and dollop a heaping tablespoon in a mound on top of the chestnut purée. Dust with cocoa, cover, and chill until required. The dessert can be made a day in advance. Serve with the meringues.

Effortlessly chic, traditionally vanilla ice cream with hot chocolate sauce and meringue, here the "dame" in question is wearing her mantle on the reverse side in the Christmas spirit of things, in other words a dark chocolate ice cream with a white chocolate sauce.

dame blanche

4 scoops of chocolate ice cream

4 meringue nests

½ cup heavy or whipping cream, whisked to fluffy peaks

cocoa for dusting

Sauce

3 ounces white chocolate, broken into pieces

¼ cup light cream

1 tablespoon Cointreau or Grand Marnier

Serves 4

To make the chocolate sauce, gently melt the chocolate, cream, and liqueur in a bowl placed over a pan with a little simmering water in it, stirring until smooth.

Remove the ice cream from the freezer 10–15 minutes before serving to allow it to soften. Place the meringue nests on four plates, with a scoop of chocolate ice cream in the center of each one, and a fluffy mound of cream on top. Dust with cocoa and serve the hot chocolate sauce separately in a little pitcher or bowl.

A rich cranberry and orange ice cream that can be made without any churning, with chocolate sauce for diehards. In fact the sauce is good for any ice cream you happen to have in the freezer. Both the sauces are optional with the parfait, which is lovely on its own too.

cranberry and orange parfait

1 cup superfine sugar

zest of 2 oranges, removed with
    a potato peeler

1 cup fresh orange juice

1½ cups cranberries

1½ cups heavy cream

9 medium egg yolks, preferably organic

Serves 8
Makes 1 x 9-inch parfait

Place the sugar and orange zest in a small saucepan with the orange juice and cranberries. Bring to a boil over medium-high heat and cook for 35–45 minutes, until you have a thick syrup (it should register 235-240°F or "soft ball" on a jam thermometer). Towards the end of this time, whisk the cream in a large bowl until stiff.

Empty the contents of the pan into a sieve placed over a bowl, pressing down on the cranberries. Put the egg yolks into a food processor and drizzle in the syrup with the motor running. Continue to whisk for a couple of minutes until the mixture turns pale and creamy, then transfer it to a large mixing bowl and stir for a minute or so until it cools to room temperature.

Whisk the cream into the egg yolk mixture in two batches, then transfer it to a 9-inch pan, cover, and freeze overnight. Remove from the freezer about 20 minutes before eating. To turn out, briefly dip the base of the terrine into a sink of hot water, run a knife around the sides, and invert. Serve in slices with the chocolate sauce and a teaspoon of the cranberry purée.

chocolate sauce

5½ ounces dark chocolate
(approx. 70% cocoa), broken
    into pieces

½ cup whole milk

¼ cup light cream

2 tablespoons Cointreau

¼ cup confectioners' sugar, sifted

Gently melt the chocolate in a bowl placed over a pan with a little simmering water in it, whisk in the milk in two batches, and then the cream, Cointreau, and sugar. Pour into a clean bowl, cover, and chill for several hours. Stir well before serving.

cranberry purée

1 cup cranberry sauce

1 tablespoon lemon juice

Gently warm the cranberry sauce in a small saucepan until it loosens, then press it through a sieve into a bowl. Stir in the lemon juice, cover, and leave to cool.

This dessert is for when you have all but given up on getting anything even vaguely healthy down your sugar-saturated offspring, although you're permitted a small shot glass of iced eau-de-vie, or other fruit brandy, poured over yours. It's a cheering Christmas-red, and plays the part turned out of a vintage gelatin mold.

cranberry delight

1½ cups cranberries

4 tablespoons fresh orange juice

½ cup superfine sugar

½ ounce (approx. 2 tablespoons)
   powdered gelatin*

approx. 2 cups cranberry juice

Serves 4–6

Place the cranberries in a small saucepan with the orange juice and sugar. Bring to a boil, then cover and cook over a low heat for 8–10 minutes, until the berries have softened. At the same time, sprinkle the powdered gelatin on to about 3 tablespoons of boiling water in a small bowl, leave for 3–4 minutes and then stir to dissolve.*

Press the contents of the pan through a sieve on top of the gelatin, and stir until it dissolves. Gradually stir in the cranberry juice, and make up to 2½ cups with a little more juice if necessary. Rinse a 2½ cup mold or bowl with water (you can also use individual molds or ramekins should you prefer). Pour in the gelatin solution and chill overnight until set.

To unmold the gelatin, briefly dip the mold into a sink of hot water, place a plate on top, and invert it.

*If the gelatin has not completely dissolved, stand the bowl in another bowl of just-boiled water for a few minutes, then stir again. Alternatively set the bowl over a pan with a little simmering water in it.

Of all the Christmas cooking to be done, it's the baking that I most enjoy—it brings the memories of my childhood Christmases flooding back. Dark afternoons spent in a warm kitchen rolling out pastry for mince pies, with the heady scent of brandy or rum, cinnamon, cloves, allspice, and ginger, and the Christmas tree shimmering in the distance, are pure pleasure. And when there are children in the house, you can cut the excitement with a knife, as the countdown to their agonizingly long wait nears its end.

Mince pies are a must in my family. But I've gone full circle on these and decided that actually I do quite like the unreconstructed type, pastry rolled that little bit too thick AND with a lid. Providing that is, it's very good pastry, short, crumbly, and sweet, and not unlike a cookie. Using half lard and half butter may make the health-conscious shudder (and there's no reason why it shouldn't be all butter), but the combination does make for meltingly flaky pastry. A plate of these also makes a great present. I try to plan a mince pie afternoon, so that I can bake up a few dozen.

A traditional Christmas cake can feel like doubling up on the mince pies, although in our house we seem to have a bottomless appetite for both. A sliver of fruit cake with farmhouse Cheddar is essential Christmas grazing. This cake is something in the way of wonder: there are no eggs, and there's no added sugar. For others, though, a very gooey festive chocolate cake may appeal more, which will double up as a dessert. And it's hard to resist a little in the way of fantasy baking—children will love this Snowmen cake with its marshmallow frosting and candies. Actually it tastes quite good too. And while you're making the mince pies, it's only one step on to a batch of spicy cookies to hang on the tree.

There is something that strokes the soul in a good old-fashioned mince pie, the kind that's passed around after Christmas carols, with a proper lid dusted with superfine sugar and that little bit too much pastry. The lard is a British touch that allows for really short pastry, and there's no need to make your own mincemeat unless you want to. These can be stored in an airtight container for up to a week, and can also be frozen.

good old-fashioned mince pies

1–2 tablespoons brandy

a squeeze of lemon juice

approx. 10½ ounces best-quality
   mincemeat

superfine sugar for dusting

Pastry

4½ cups all-purpose flour

½ cup unsalted butter, chilled
   and diced

½ cup lard, chilled and diced

¾ cup confectioners' sugar, sifted

1 medium egg yolk

milk or water, to brush the top

Makes approx. 18

To make the pastry, place the flour, butter, and lard in a food processor, give it a quick burst at high speed to reduce it to a crumb-like consistency, then add the confectioners' sugar and give it another quick burst. Add the egg yolk and enough milk or water to bring the dough together, wrap it in plastic wrap, and chill for 1 hour or overnight.

Preheat the oven to 375°F. Stir the brandy and lemon juice into the mincemeat. Roll two-thirds of the pastry to ¼ inch thickness on a lightly floured work surface, and cut out circles using a 3-inch fluted cutter to fit a couple of muffin pans (ideally non-stick). Place these in the pans and fill with a heaping teaspoon of mincemeat.

Roll out the remaining pastry with the trimmings and cut out lids using a 2½-inch fluted cutter. Brush the rim of the pies with milk or water, lay the lids on top, and gently press the edges together. Dust with sugar and bake for 15–20 minutes, until the pastry is a pale gold. Serve warm, about 20 minutes out of the oven, or at room temperature. They can also be reheated for 5 minutes in an oven preheated to 325°F. A little brandy butter (see page 128) on top or slipped under the lid while they're warm keeps them in traditional mode, with or without the rum sauce.

Unless you are planning on taking a two-week break before the big day, the chances are you won't have time to make a gingerbread house. But we can have mini iced ginger cakes with little in the way of fuss, it's the essential spice that we're after.

mini gingerbread cakes

4 tablespoons beer
½ cup dark brown sugar
⅛ teaspoon baking soda
⅔ cup self-rising flour
1 level teaspoon ground ginger
1 medium egg
3 tablespoons peanut
  or vegetable oil
fine white royal icing

Makes approx. 15

Preheat the oven to 350°F, and arrange about fifteen paper mini muffin liners in one or two mini muffin pans. Alternatively arrange double liners, one inside the other, on a baking sheet. Bring the beer and sugar to a boil in a small saucepan, working out any lumps with the back of a spoon. Remove from the heat and stir in the baking soda, then set aside while you prepare the cake batter.

Sift the flour and ginger into a bowl. Whisk together the egg and oil in another bowl, then slowly add this to the flour, stirring. Add the beer mixture in two batches, gently mixing it in. Fill each muffin case three-quarters and bake for approx. 15 minutes, until risen, firm, and starting to color. Remove and leave them to cool, then decorate with a zigzag of spidery white icing and little icing dots. These cakes will keep well in an airtight container for several days.

These individual fruitcakes with a buttery crumble on top will appeal to those who find the typical Christmas fruitcake a little bit too dark and full of dried fruits. These are delicious eaten slightly warm, with a dollop of rum or brandy butter (see page 128).

christmas crumble muffins

Crumble

⅓ cup light brown sugar

5 tablespoons unsalted butter, chilled and diced

1 cup all-purpose flour

⅓ teaspoon ground cinnamon

Cake

¾ cup unsalted butter, diced

1 cup light brown sugar

3 medium eggs, plus 1 yolk

3 tablespoons dark rum

½ cup currants

⅓ cup diced candied peel

⅓ cup undyed glacé cherries, sliced

1 ¾ cups all-purpose flour

¾ teaspoon baking powder

confectioners' sugar for dusting

Makes 12

Preheat the oven to 375°F, and arrange twelve paper muffin liners in a muffin pan. Place all the ingredients for the crumble in the bowl of a food processor and blend to fine crumbs, then transfer the mixture to a bowl.

To make the cake mixture, place the butter and sugar in the bowl of a food processor and beat for several minutes until fluffy. Add the eggs and the yolk one at a time, scraping down the bowl if necessary, then incorporate the rum (don't worry if the mixture appears curdled at this point). Transfer to a large bowl. Toss the currants, peel, and cherries with a little flour to coat them. Sift the remaining flour and baking powder over the cake mixture and gently fold in, followed by the dried and candied fruits.

Spoon the cake mixture into the paper liners, half filling them, and scatter the crumble over the top. Bake the cakes for 25 minutes, until risen and lightly golden on the surface. Leave to cool, then dust with confectioners' sugar. These are at their yummiest the day they are made, when the crumble is crisp, but they can also be stored for a day or two. A plastic food bag, loosely tied, is preferable to an airtight container.

Dense, fudgy chocolate cakes are ever the hallmark of luxury, and this won't let you down, with its hint of hazelnuts and rum or coffee in what is otherwise full-on chocolate.

chocolate fudge drizzle cake

Cake

1 cup unsalted butter, diced

7 ounces dark chocolate (approx. 50% cocoa), broken into pieces

3 tablespoons dark rum, espresso, or strong black coffee

4 medium eggs, separated

⅔ cup light brown sugar

½ cup ground almonds

½ teaspoon sea salt

¼ cup hazelnuts, peeled

confectioners' sugar for dusting

Icing

2 tablespoons dark brown sugar

1 tablespoon heavy cream

1 ounce dark chocolate, broken into pieces

2 tablespoons unsalted butter

Makes 1 x 8-inch cake

Preheat the oven to 350°F, and butter an 8-inch round cake pan, 3½ inches deep with a removable base. Melt the butter, chocolate, and rum or coffee in a bowl placed over a pan of simmering water, stirring occasionally. Whisk the egg whites in a bowl until stiff, then gradually whisk in half the sugar, a tablespoon at a time, whisking for about 20 seconds with each addition, until by the end you have a stiff, glossy meringue. Whisk the egg yolks with the remaining sugar in a large bowl for several minutes until pale and doubled in volume. Transfer the mixture to a bowl.

Fold the chocolate and butter into the egg and sugar mixture, lightly fold in the ground almonds with the salt, then fold in the egg whites in two batches. Pour the mixture into the prepared pan, give it a couple of taps on the work surface to bring up any large air bubbles, and bake for 40–45 minutes until a skewer inserted into the center comes out clean. Run a knife around the edge of the cake and leave it to cool in the pan. Meanwhile, spread the nuts over the base of a small baking dish and toast for about 15 minutes until golden. Leave to cool and then coarsely chop.

Invert the cake onto a plate and remove the base (you will be decorating the bottom rather than the top). To make the icing, heat the brown sugar and cream together for several minutes in a bowl placed over a pan of simmering water, until completely smooth. Add the chocolate and butter and continue to heat, whisking until glossy and blended. Trickle the icing over the cake, so that it runs down the sides as well, and scatter the nuts on top. Leave to set for a couple of hours. It will keep well in a covered container for several days. You may like to give it a light dusting of confectioners' sugar before serving.

all gold christmas cake

Homemade marzipan is as delicate and pretty as commercial marzipan is overpowering and garish. The real thing has a restrained scent of almonds, the gentlest hint of brandy and lemon, and is a pale ivory in color. In fact there's no need for icing at all, I'd stop right there. But I would invest in a small container of edible gold powder, which is available from cake specialists (see page 9). It lasts for years, so you can put it away with the tree decorations and get it out again next year.

This is a lovely moist and sticky fruit cake that draws all its sweetness from dates and dried fruits. It will appeal to those who like really dark fruitcakes. Feed it with teasing teaspoons of Calvados or brandy in the run-up to Christmas, so it becomes richer and deeper by the week. Peeling back the layers of crinkly parchment paper and drawing in its heady scent is a special ritual. That said, it can also be eaten immediately, but otherwise, if you're heeding tradition on "Stir-up Sunday" and making a Christmas pudding, why not make this cake at the same time?

1⅓ cups unsalted butter

2 cups apple juice

2 cups pitted and chopped dates

2⅓ cups raisins

2 cups golden raisins

1 teaspoon baking soda

1½ cups all-purpose flour, sifted

1¾ cups ground almonds

½ teaspoon freshly grated nutmeg

½ teaspoon ground cinnamon

finely grated zest of 1 orange
    and 1 lemon

approx. 2 tablespoons Calvados or brandy,
    for feeding the cake

Marzipan

½ cup ground almonds

1½ cups confectioners' sugar

1 teaspoon lemon juice

1 teaspoon Calvados or brandy

1 medium organic egg white

Decoration

½ cup apricot jam

edible gold powder, a thick gold ribbon,
    strings of gold beads (optional)

Makes 1 x 8-inch cake

Melt the butter in a medium-size saucepan with the apple juice, then stir in the dates, raisins, and golden raisins, bring to a boil, and simmer over low heat for 5 minutes. Transfer the mixture to a large mixing bowl and stir in the baking soda (the mixture will sizzle furiously), then leave it to cool for 10 minutes.

Preheat the oven to 325°F, and butter an 8-inch round cake pan, 3½ inches deep, with a removable base. Line the bottom with parchment paper, and butter this also. Beat the flour, ground almonds, nutmeg, and cinnamon into the dried fruit mixture. Fold in the zest and transfer the mixture to the cake pan, smoothing the surface.

Tear off a sheet of parchment paper large enough to cover the surface of the cake and go about halfway down the outside of the pan. Cut out a small circle from the center about ¾ inch in diameter, then butter the surface that will come in contact with the cake as it rises. Lay it over the top of the pan and tie it in place with string. Bake the cake for 2½ hours, until a skewer inserted into the center comes out clean—it will be a very deep brown at this point. Leave the cake to cool, then run a knife around the collar, remove it from the base, and peel off the bottom paper.

The cake will be good to eat from the following day onwards. If maturing it, however, pierce the top all over with a skewer and feed it with a teaspoon of Calvados or brandy, then wrap it in a double layer of new parchment paper and then foil. Continue to feed it at weekly intervals for about 6 weeks. You can step the liquor up to a couple of teaspoons at a time if maturing it for a few weeks only.

To make the marzipan, place all the ingredients except the egg white in the bowl of a food processor and blend together, then add the egg white and mix together into a pliable paste. Wrap the marzipan in plastic wrap and chill until required. Hang on to the bowl that contained the egg white, as you need just a little for the decoration.

Gently heat the jam in a small saucepan, press it through a sieve, and very lightly glaze the cake using a pastry brush—again hang on to the bowl. Measure the cake from the base of one side to the base of the other. Thinly roll out the marzipan on a work surface dusted with confectioners' sugar into a circle a little bigger than this, about 12 inches in diameter. Loosen it with an offset spatula every now and then, and dust the surface with confectioners' sugar as necessary, but avoid dusting the top. Roll the marzipan around the rolling pin, lift it up, and carefully lay it on top of the cake, letting it drape down the sides. Press it to the sides of the cake, cut out darts where folds appear, and smooth these with your fingers, then trim it at base level.

Roll out the trimmings and cut out about three holly leaves using a cookie cutter or template, and make little balls as berries. Dab a little jam on to the base of these using the residual jam in the bowl and arrange on top of the cake. Brush the tops of the balls and the edge of the leaves with a little of the egg white left in the bowl, using a small brush, and dust with gold powder, again using a fine brush. Tie a big gold ribbon around the outside, and some strings of gold beads should you have any. Set the cake aside and leave overnight for the marzipan to semi-dry, then store in an airtight container.

This cake is my way of sneaking a poinsettia into the house, as they don't really feature on my landscape architect husband's radar. But he probably wouldn't mind eating it, a moist hazelnut sponge cake with a moussey cinnamon butter icing.

You can tone it down still further by making the flowers with white icing. But for the full on effect it's either red icing, or you can make the flowers by kneading about a teaspoon of red food coloring into 7 ounces of marzipan to dye it pink. Thinly roll this out on a work surface lightly dusted with confectioners' sugar, cut out poinsettia leaves, and decorate the cake. Using fine red royal icing, trace in the outside of the leaves and the veins.

poinsettia cake

Sponge
¾ pound roasted chopped hazelnuts*
6 medium eggs, separated
1⅓ cups superfine sugar
1½ teaspoons baking powder

Filling
7 tablespoons unsalted butter, softened
⅓ cup confectioners' sugar
½ teaspoon ground cinnamon
½ cup thick custard

Icing and Decoration
1¼ pounds marzipan icing (see pages
   158–160)
½ cup apricot jam
gold, red, green, or white ribbon
   and gold balls to decorate

Makes 1 x 8-inch cake

To prepare the sponge, preheat the oven to 400°F, and butter two 8-inch round cake pans at least 1½ inches deep with a removable base. Grind the nuts in batches in a coffee grinder, taking care to stop the motor before they turn to a paste at the bottom. Whisk the egg yolks and sugar together in a large bowl—the mixture should not be too pale and thick. Stiffly whisk the egg whites and gently fold them into the mixture in three turns. Fold in the ground nuts and the baking powder.

Divide the cake mixture between the pans and give them a couple of taps on the work surface to bring up any air bubbles. Bake for approximately 25 minutes, until the top feels springy to the touch and the cake is shrinking away from the sides. A skewer inserted into the center should come out clean. Remove the collar from the cakes and leave to cool.

Using an hand mixer, beat the softened butter in a medium-size bowl until creamy and almost white. If it's on the hard side you can beat it in a food processor first. Sift the sugar and cinnamon over the butter and fold in, then gradually whisk in the custard and continue whisking for another few minutes, on a low speed to begin with and then on a higher speed, until it is fluffy and mousse-like.

If the sides of the cakes are particularly high, trim the edges with a bread knife. Remove the sponges from their bases and invert them, then spread the top of one with the filling and sandwich with the second one. Measure the cake from the base of one side to the base of the other. Thinly roll out 1 pound of the marzipan icing on a work surface dusted with confectioners' sugar into a circle a little bigger than this, about 14 inches in diameter. Loosen it with an offset spatula every now and then, and dust the surface with confectioners' sugar as necessary, but avoid dusting the top.

Gently heat the jam in a small saucepan until it liquefies, press it through a sieve, and use it to brush the top and sides of the cake. Roll the icing around the rolling pin, lift it up, and carefully drape over the cake, pressing it to the sides. Cut out darts from the side where there is excess icing and smooth the edges together, then trim the base.

Cut out a poinsettia leaf about 3 inches in length from a piece of paper (if in doubt about their shape, then google an image, or refer to a Christmas card). Roll out the remaining icing as thinly as possible in the same way as before, and cut out some leaves. Use these to decorate the top of the cake, securing them with a little jam. Tie a thick ribbon around the outside. The cake will keep well for several days in a cool place, loosely covered with plastic wrap, or in an airtight container.

*You can also use ground almonds, or ground toasted almonds. Arrange almond flakes in a thin layer on baking sheets and toast for 9–10 minutes at 350°F, then cool. These, however, tend to be a little oilier when you grind them.

"It's a marshmallow world in the winter," or so we wish. This is one to have fun with—decorate it with marshmallow snowmen, chocolate coins, and candy canes and it will be every child's idea of a dream Christmas cake. But otherwise raid the candy store for jelly beans, marshmallows, and licorice. White marshmallows will give a suitably snowy frosting, and pink ones a pale Barbie-doll blush.

snowmen cake

Cake

½ pound unsalted butter, diced

1¼ cups superfine sugar

2 cups self-rising flour

2 teaspoons baking powder

finely grated zest of 1 orange

4 medium eggs

½ cup fresh smooth orange juice

Frosting

2 medium organic egg whites

¾ cup superfine sugar

2 tablespoons fresh smooth
    orange juice

½ teaspoon cream of tartar

pinch of sea salt

11 pink or white marshmallows, halved

selection of marshmallows, chocolate
    coins, and candy canes to decorate

Makes 1 x 8-inch cake

Preheat the oven to 325°F, and butter an 8-inch round cake pan, 3½ inches deep, with a removable base. Place all the cake ingredients in the bowl of a food processor and beat together. Transfer the mixture to the cake pan, smoothing the surface, and bake for 50–55 minutes, or until a skewer inserted into the center comes out clean. Run a knife around the collar of the cake and leave it to cool. You can leave the cake on the base or remove it as you prefer.

To make the frosting, blend the egg whites, sugar, orange juice, cream of tartar, and salt in a large bowl, using a hand blender. Place the bowl over a pan with a little simmering water in it and whisk at high speed for 5 minutes, until you have a thick, mousse-like glaze that stands in peaks. Add the marshmallows and stir for several minutes until they begin to soften and melt, then whisk until the mixture is smooth and they have completely melted, and remove from the heat.

Spread the frosting thickly over the top and sides of the cake using an offset spatula, though you may not need quite all of it. Decorate with the candies and set aside for a couple of hours. The cake will keep well for several days in an airtight container.

A bûche de Noël is the French equivalent of the English Christmas pudding, and in typical style has glamorous all-around potential, like so much of their pâtisserie.

bûche de noël

Sponge

½ cup cocoa
a pinch of sea salt
3 large eggs
⅓ cup light brown sugar

Filling

3 ounces dark chocolate (approx.
   70% cocoa), broken into pieces
13 ounces unsweetened chestnut
   purée
⅓ cup light brown sugar
1½ teaspoons vanilla extract
¾ cup whipping cream

Christmas figurines to decorate
confectioners' sugar for dusting

Serves 6–8

To make the sponge, preheat the oven to 350°F. Butter a 9½ x 13-inch jellyroll pan, line it with parchment paper and butter this also. Sift the cocoa into a bowl and add the salt. Place the eggs and brown sugar in a bowl and whisk for 8–10 minutes, using a hand blender, until the mixture is mousse-like. Lightly fold in the cocoa in two turns. Pour the mixture into the prepared pan and smooth it using an offset spatula. Give the pan a couple of sharp taps on the work surface to eliminate any large air bubbles and bake the sponge for 8–10 minutes, until set and springy to touch.

Lay out a kitchen towel and sift a fine layer of confectioners' sugar over it. Tip the cake out on to it and carefully roll the cake up in the kitchen towel, with the paper, starting at the short end so you end up with a short fat roll. Leave to cool for 40–60 minutes.

To make the filling, gently melt the chocolate in a bowl placed over a pan of simmering water, then cool to room temperature. Cream the chestnut purée, sugar, and vanilla in a food processor, then add the chocolate. Whip the cream until it forms soft peaks, and fold it into the chocolate chestnut mixture in two batches.

Carefully unroll the sponge and peel off the paper parchment. Spread with half the chocolate chestnut filling, then roll the sponge up again and transfer it on to a long serving plate, seam downward. You could also line a small board with silver foil and decorate the edge. Smooth the rest of the filling on top, then make lines along its length with a fork, swirling the ends to create a log effect, and making a few knots on the log too. Decorate it with your favorite Christmas figurines.

Chill the roulade for an hour; if keeping it for longer than this, loosely cover it with plastic wrap and bring it back to room temperature for 30 minutes before eating.

A guiding light for Santa as well as the Magi, we leave these out with the essential sip of something fiery or a glass of milk and a pile of moss for the reindeer on Christmas Eve.

star of bethlehem cookies

1½ cups all-purpose flour

⅓ cup superfine sugar

8 tablespoons unsalted butter, diced

¼ teaspoon vanilla extract

1 medium egg yolk, beaten

1½ tablespoons cocoa, sifted

peanut or vegetable oil for brushing

¾ ounce dark chocolate (approx. 70% cocoa), broken into pieces

confectioners' sugar for dusting (optional)

Makes approx. 15

Place half of the flour, half the sugar, and half the butter in the bowl of a food processor and briefly blend until the mixture is crumb-like. Add the vanilla and half the egg yolk and blend again until the mixture comes together into a ball. Wrap in plastic wrap and chill for at least an hour. Make a second batch of dough in the same way except adding the cocoa to the food processor with the flour (and omitting any vanilla). Chill this too.

Preheat the oven to 375°F, and brush a couple of cookie sheets with oil. Thinly roll out each dough in turn on a lightly floured work surface, rotating it as necessary, very lightly sprinkling the top with a little flour to stop the rolling pin from sticking. Cut out stars using a 2½-inch cutter and arrange on cookie sheets, rolling the dough twice. Bake for approx. 10 minutes, until lightly colored, then remove and immediately loosen with a metal spatula—if you leave them even a few minutes they will break as you remove them. Leave to cool.

Gently melt the chocolate in a small saucepan over low heat. Using a pastry brush, dab a little in the center of each vanilla cookie, then sandwich with a chocolate one so the points of the stars are alternated. If you like, lightly dust the tops with confectioners' sugar, using a strainer. Set aside in a cool place for about an hour for the chocolate to harden. These will keep well in an airtight container for several days.

Hanging the tree with spiced cookies is one of those Martha Stewart moments that we are inclined to experience at this time of year, however lapsed we may be during the rest of it. The good bit being that you can get your children to make them: older ones can do the baking while younger ones can decorate them. But it's worth saving the hanging until Christmas Eve or just before, not only to keep them fresh, as they soften within a day, but because otherwise, as with tree chocolates, the tree will have been denuded by Christmas Day.

You will need a set of cutters, anything from holly leaves, bells, snowflakes, snowmen, stockings, and stars (see page 9 for sources). Also some thin ribbon for hanging them.

christmas tree cookies

3½ tablespoons unsalted butter
½ cup superfine sugar
¼ cup honey
2¼ cups all-purpose flour
½ teaspoon baking powder
½ teaspoon baking soda
1 teaspoon each ground ginger
   and cinnamon
½ beaten medium egg
vegetable oil for brushing
white royal icing to decorate
silver balls (optional)

Makes 20–30

Gently heat the butter, sugar, and honey together in a small saucepan, stirring until melted and smooth. Working off the heat, add the dry ingredients and stir until crumbly, then add the egg and work to a dough. If it seems very sticky you can add a little more flour. Transfer this to a work surface, form it into a ball, then pat it between your palms until you have a pleasingly smooth and shiny dough. Wrap it in plastic wrap, leave to cool, then chill for several hours or overnight.

Preheat the oven to 350°F, and brush a couple of cookie sheets with vegetable oil. Thinly roll out the dough on a lightly floured work surface to an 1/8-inch thickness and cut out the desired shapes using cookie cutters. Roll the dough twice, arranging the cookies on the cookie sheets—they don't spread much, so you can place them quite close together. If you are planning on hanging them, make a hole at the top of each one using a skewer.

Bake the cookies for 10–12 minutes until an even pale gold; the lower sheet may take longer than the upper one. The holes will have closed up a little, so make them a bit larger using the skewer. Now loosen the cookies with an offset spatula—it's important to do this immediately before they harden and become brittle. Transfer to a rack to cool. Ice and decorate them as you like, and leave to set for an hour or two. They can be stored in an airtight container, un-iced or iced, for several weeks. Thread them with thin ribbon if you are planning on hanging them.

Just when you thought it was all over, another cake, traditionally served in France on Epiphany to celebrate the arrival of the Magi in Bethlehem to honor the baby Jesus. It is also known as Twelfth Night cake. Just as we hide a coin in our Christmas pudding, a small figurine known as "la fève" is inserted into the filling (most likely plastic these days), and whoever finds it in their slice is crowned king for a day, which when there are children present means some discreet digging around on the part of whoever is serving it to make sure it goes to the right person. I usually dish this up for New Year's Eve dinner, when the kings are still journeying, as the cake is served in the few days up to and beyond Epiphany. And with it a spoonful of whipped cream, brandy butter, or the rum sauce on page 128.

galette des rois

9 tablespoons unsalted butter, softened
⅔ cup superfine sugar
1¼ cups ground almonds
½ cup all-purpose flour
finely grated zest of 1 lemon
2 medium eggs
1 tablespoon dark rum (optional)
1 tablespoon milk
approx. 13 ounces puff pastry

Serves 6–8

Preheat the oven to 425°F. To make the filling, blend the butter, sugar, and ground almonds in a food processor, then add the flour, lemon zest, one of the eggs, and an egg white, and the rum if including. You should have a creamy spreadable paste. Blend the remaining egg yolk with the milk.

Thinly roll out half the pastry on a lightly floured work surface to a thickness of about ⅛ inch, and cut out a 10-inch circle using a plate as a guide. Spread the filling to within 1 inch of the edge. If you like you can push a little figure or a coin into the mixture. Roll out the second half of the pastry 1 inch larger all round than the first circle. Paint the lower rim with egg wash, lay the second pastry circle on top and press the edges together, then trim the top circle level with the lower one. Paint the pie all over with the egg wash and fold in the rim, then paint this too. Mark the surface with the prongs of a fork in diagonal lines, and the rim, and cut a slit in the surface to allow the steam to escape.

Bake the pie for 20 minutes until golden and risen. Serve warm about 15 minutes out of the oven. It can also be reheated for about 20 minutes at 325°F.

chocolates
and gifts

Beautiful chocolates are central to holiday celebrations. In fact one of the first signs that Christmas is upon us is the windows of French pâtisseries, dressed to the nines, which hold the food-obsessed among us in awe in the run-up with every espresso stop we make. It's not so much the twinkling display of lights strung all around town that draws our eyes as the tiny gold- and silver-wrapped chocolates, shimmering sugared almonds, marzipan figurines of snowmen and Santa, and striped candy canes and lollipops. And we intend to have all of these.

Homemade truffles come top of my list if I'm going to get melting. These couldn't be easier, especially when they are square as opposed to round, and don't call for rolling. Add a drop of your favorite hooch—pretty much anything goes with chocolate, so design them with the receiver in mind. Brandy and rum are ever Christmassy, but more normally I surreptitiously spirit a few tablespoons of whatever fine whisky or Calvados my husband's got in the liquor cabinet. And unlike so many store-bought truffles, here you can guarantee a really good high percentage cocoa chocolate.

The modern fad of chocolate slabs is also welcome. These couldn't be prettier or easier, and can be themed in any number of festive ways, with dried cranberries and sour cherries, slivers of candied peel, walnuts, and toasted hazelnuts, Brazil nuts, glacé cherries, or with a Christmas tree traced in M&Ms, a snowman, or a stocking.

Homemade chocolates make great presents, as do jars of chutneys and herb jellies. They're bound to be appreciated with all those impromptu lunches of the end of the roast with some salads, that are given a second life with a lovely relish of some sort. Even more luxurious is a clementine curd spiked with Cointreau, so deliciously decadent the morning after Christmas with some toasted brioche or warm croissants.

My granny had a fondness for chocolate violets, ginger wine, and liquid-filled jellies, so these take me back. And they're very pretty, though be sure to use a low-percentage cocoa dark chocolate rather than a high one, which will bloom.

violet medallions

3½ ounces dark chocolate (approx. 50% cocoa), broken into pieces
1 ounce white chocolate, broken into pieces
crystallized violets

Makes approx. 25

Gently melt the two chocolates separately in bowls placed over pans with a little simmering water in them. At the same time, tear off a large sheet of parchment paper, and draw circles about 1½ inches in diameter on it (I use a tealight as a guide). Turn the paper over on the work surface and spread about half a teaspoon of dark chocolate inside each circle, using the outline to shape it. If the white chocolate has started to set again, gently reheat it. Drop a small dot in the center of the dark chocolate, and swirl it using a toothpick. Place a crystallized violet in the center. Leave the discs to harden completely in a cool place for an hour or two. Peel the medallions off the paper, and store in an airtight container—they will be good for several days.

The milk chocolate drizzle is gooier than the dark chocolate base, a little like the inside of a truffle, which gives a lovely contrast. And the decoration could be anything graphic that takes your imagination. But the Christmas tree with silvery lights should melt any heart.

swirled slab

1 pound dark chocolate
  (approx. 50% cocoa), broken
  into pieces
3½ ounces milk chocolate, broken
  into pieces
2 tablespoons strong black coffee
M&Ms or white chocolate buttons,
  and silver or colored balls
  to decorate

Makes 1 x 13 x 10-inch slab

Gently melt the dark and milk chocolate in separate bowls over pans with a little simmering water in them. Blend the coffee into the milk chocolate a tablespoon at a time, which will darken it in color. Line the base of a 13 x 10-inch jellyroll pan with plastic wrap. Pour the dark chocolate over the base, smoothing the surface, and drizzle the milk chocolate on top in swirls. Once you are confident the chocolate is completely cool, use M&Ms or white buttons to make a Christmas tree standing in a container in the center of the slab, and scatter some balls in between the buttons to create the effect of twinkling lights. Set aside in a cool place to harden for several hours.

To serve, carefully remove the plastic wrap on the base, and place on a board or plate. Serve it with coffee. It keeps well for several days.

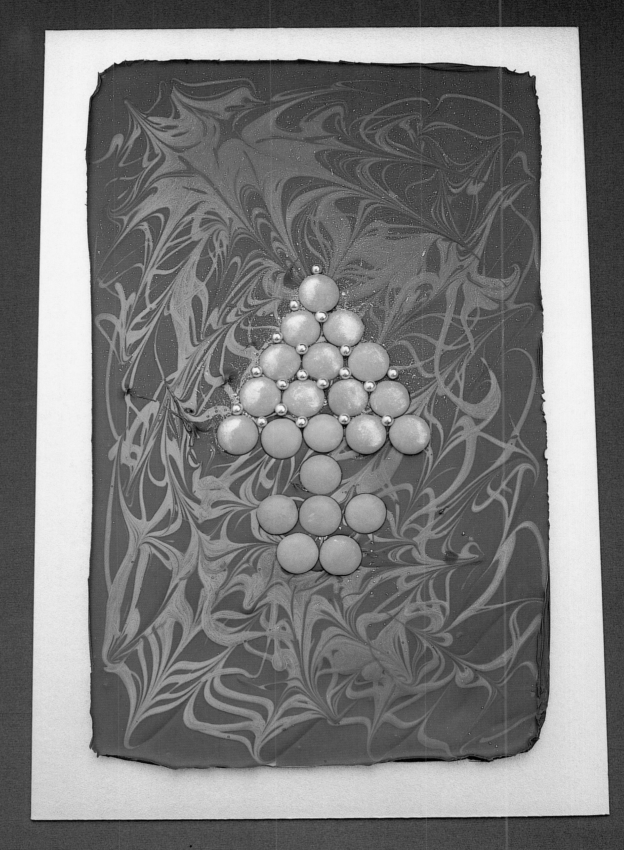

If you have ever tried to make florentines you will know they are much harder to get right than their appearance suggests. This simple slab has all the treasures for which we love them, in particular that toffee almond brittle. At this time of year there are some gorgeous candied peels to take advantage of—try to buy it by the segment and slice it yourself.

florentine slab

⅓ cup almond flakes

14 ounces dark chocolate (approx. 50% cocoa), broken into pieces

½ cup superfine sugar

⅓ cup undyed glacé cherries, halved

¼ cup candied orange peel, cut into thin slivers about ¾ inch long

Makes 1 x 13 x 10-inch slab

Preheat the oven to 400°F. Spread the almonds out in a thin layer in a shallow baking dish and toast for 8–10 minutes, until lightly golden, then remove from the oven and leave to cool.

Line a 13 x 10-inch jellyroll pan with plastic wrap. Gently melt the chocolate in a bowl placed over a pan with a little simmering water in it, removing the bowl now and then and stir to avoid overheating. Smooth the melted chocolate over the base of the pan.

At the same time place the sugar and ¼ cup of water in a small saucepan, bring to a boil and simmer over low heat for about 15 minutes until a deep gold, swirling it occasionally as it starts to color to ensure it caramelizes evenly. Stir in the nuts. Scatter nut clusters over the surface of the chocolate, then scatter the cherries and candied peel on top. Set aside in a cool place for several hours to set. The slab should keep for a couple of days; it will still taste good beyond this, but may develop a bloom. Set aside, and avoid covering as trapped moisture will cause the chocolate to bloom.

There are some beautiful nougats on the market, ones with dried raspberries and blueberries and other goodies in them.

nougat cups

½ cup heavy cream
3½ ounces dark chocolate (approx.
   70% cocoa), broken into pieces
½ teaspoon vanilla extract
5½ ounces nougat, cut into small bits
silver or gold balls, or chocolate
   shavings to decorate (optional)

Makes approx. 20

Arrange about twenty paper mini-muffin or candy liners on a small tray or in a roasting pan. Bring the cream to a boil in a small non-stick saucepan. Pour it over the chocolate in a bowl, leave for a minute or two, and then give it a stir, and repeat this until the chocolate has completely melted and you have a thick cream. Stir in the vanilla, then fold in the nougat bits.

Fill the paper liners with the mixture—if you like you can scatter a few silver or gold balls, or chocolate shavings on top. Loosely cover with plastic wrap and chill for a few hours. These should keep well for about a week in the fridge.

If you're married to a whisky lover, as I am, you're unlikely to get much of a sip from that fine bottle of single malt that comes his way over Christmas. I insist on being left my angel's share or the near equivalent, a wee bit for some chocolate truffles. The last such fine bottle was a seventeen-year-old Highland single malt whisky from the Adelphi distillery, which specializes in rare whiskies.

These truffles take the easy way out—we can't be having all that rolling and dipping demanded by round ones. With this method, for the sake of some ten minutes' labor, you end up with a large bowl of meltingly creamy square truffles.

whisky galore truffles

1¾ cup heavy cream
14 ounces dark chocolate
   (approx. 70% cocoa), broken
   into pieces
2 tablespoons whisky, ideally
   single malt
approx. 3½ tablespoons cocoa

Makes almost 2 pounds

Bring the cream to a boil in a small non-stick saucepan. Pour it over the chocolate in a bowl, leave for a minute or two and then give it a stir, then repeat this until the chocolate has completely melted and you have a thick cream. Stir in the whisky.

Next you want a square or oblong baking pan in which to set a slab just under ¾ inch in depth. I use a 10-inch square brownie pan, and end up with a rectangle about 6 x 10 inches. First line the pan with plastic wrap, with plenty overhanging the sides, enough to fold one end back over the top of the slab once you pour it in. Pour the chocolate into one end of the pan, allowing it to spread towards the other, and fold the plastic wrap at this end back over the slab, so you have a rectangle about 6 x 10 x ¼ inch, smoothing the surface with your fingers. Tuck the plastic wrap ends underneath the pan to keep the slab in place and chill for several hours until set.

Sift the cocoa into a large bowl, and turn the slab out on to a work surface. Trim the edges and cut into ½-inch cubes. Place about a third of these in the bowl, and swirl to coat them in cocoa. Remove them with your hands, giving them a little shake in your palm to dust off any excess cocoa, then pile into a large bowl, or bowls, and repeat with the remainder. Cover and chill until required, removing them from the fridge about 30 minutes before eating. They will keep for several days—you can always dust them with a little more cocoa if it seems to have been absorbed.

The perfect chutney to serve with leftover duck and goose, and equally good with turkey and the cheeseboard. You can dip in as soon as it's made, or let it mature for a few months. Clip-top jars are ideal, and like most chutneys this is a good keeper.

fig, star anise, and port chutney

4½ cups ready-to-eat dried figs, stalks trimmed, sliced

1 pound eating apples, quartered, cored, and diced

1½ pounds red onions, peeled, halved, and sliced

3 star anise

6 green cardamom pods

1 x 3 inch cinnamon stick

2 cups red wine vinegar

1⅔ cups apple juice

2¼ cups light brown sugar

1 tablespoon sea salt

½ cup port

Makes approx. 6 cups

Place the figs, apples, and onions in a large pot. Add the spices, wrapping the star anise and cardamom in a small square of muslin or cotton, for ease of removing them at the end. Add the vinegar then the apple juice, sugar, and salt and stir, then bring to a simmer and cook over a low heat for 3–3½ hours, adding the port about an hour before the end of cooking. Stir occasionally, but more frequently towards the end to prevent the chutney from sticking.

It's difficult to specify exactly how long the chutney will take to cook, as this will depend on the size of your pot and the heat at which you simmer it. Don't worry about paying too much attention at the beginning, but keep a watchful eye towards the end. There should still be a small amount of sticky syrup floating on the surface, bearing in mind the chutney will get firm on cooling. To test it, spread a couple of tablespoons on a cold plate, leave it to cool for a few minutes, then judge whether it is the right consistency. Once the chutney is cooked, discard the spices.

Heat three 2-cup clip-top jars (or whatever jars you are using) for 5 minutes in a medium hot oven (about 375°F). Fill the hot jars with the hot chutney, then close them and leave to cool.

There is something slightly risqué about this curd, which makes it so apt for spreading on toast for breakfast during the festive season. You can also use it to fill little puff pastries for dessert. As curd has a limited shelf life, share this with several friends, dividing it into small containers or jars.

clementine curd with cointreau

juice of 2 clementines
finely grated zest and juice
  of ½ lemon
2 tablespoons Cointreau
6 medium eggs, preferably organic
¾ cup unsalted butter, diced
1½ cups superfine sugar

Makes 2-2½ cups

Heat all the ingredients in a small non-stick saucepan over low heat, whisking constantly until the butter melts. Continue to stir with a wooden spoon until it thickens into a custard. While this takes time, it happens very quickly at the end, so it's worth being patient. Care must be taken that it doesn't boil, otherwise it will curdle, but don't worry if it seems slightly lumpy.

Pass the curd through a sieve into a bowl, then divide between jars or small containers. Cover, and chill once cool, when it will set. It will keep well for at least a couple of weeks if stored in the fridge.

A colorful and chunky piccalilli that can be eaten as soon as it is made.
Sprinkle it with chopped cilantro and serve it like a little salad side dish.

chunky piccalilli

2 tablespoons extra virgin olive oil

1 red pepper, core and seeds removed,
    cut into ½-inch strips

1 cup cauliflower florets, stalks trimmed

⅔ cup romanesco broccoli florets

4 fresh medium-hot red chiles, left whole

2 medium carrots, ends removed, peeled,
    and cut into 8 sticks each

6 shallots, peeled

2 tablespoons cider
    or white wine vinegar

2 cups white wine

½ cup water

2 teaspoons ground ginger

1 teaspoon turmeric

2 teaspoons superfine sugar

1 bay leaf

1½ teaspoons sea salt

2 teaspoons cornstarch, blended
    with 1 tablespoon water

2 teaspoons wholegrain mustard

Makes 4-5 cups

Heat the olive oil in a large pot over medium heat. Add all the vegetables and fry for a few minutes, stirring occasionally. Add the vinegar, wine, and water, the spices, sugar, bay leaf, and salt, then bring to a boil and simmer over low heat for 20 minutes, stirring occasionally. Stir in the cornstarch paste and simmer for a couple of minutes longer until the sauce thickens. Stir in the mustard, transfer to a bowl, and leave to cool.

If you are planning on eating the piccalilli within a few hours, cover and set aside somewhere cool. If you are keeping it for a few days, chill and bring it back to room temperature before serving. If, however, you are making it for a present or want to bottle it, first sterilize your jars. Wash and dry them, then place them in an oven preheated to 375°F, for 5 minutes. Remove and fill with the hot vegetables, packing them down, then pour the liquid on top. Seal the jars with their lids and leave to cool completely. Store in the fridge for up to a month.

Shimmering herb jellies make a lovely present over Christmas, and are almost certain to make a welcome appearance at the table at some point during the festivities, with some cold meat.

herb jelly

3½ pounds cooking apples
1½ cups cider vinegar
fresh rosemary sprigs
  (2 ounces)
4 cups granulated sugar

Makes 5-6 cups

Cut the unpeeled, uncored apples into pieces and place in a large pot with the vinegar, 3 cups of water, and half the rosemary. Bring to a boil, then simmer over very low heat for 1 hour. Now transfer the contents of the pot into a jelly bag* suspended over a large bowl—I find it easiest to fill the bag in the bowl before lifting it up. Leave to drip through for at least a couple of hours, or overnight. You should end up with a cloudy pink juice. Don't actually squeeze the bag or you will jeopardize the next stage, when the juice clarifies.

Place a few little dishes or saucers in the freezer. Measure the juice into a large pot—you should have about 3 cups. Add 2½ cups of sugar for every 3 cups of juice. Bring to a boil, stirring occasionally until the sugar melts, and simmer for 15 minutes. Meanwhile, preheat the oven to 375°F, and sterilize your open jars for 5 minutes. These should be warm when you fill them. Skim the rubbery white scum off the jelly. To test whether it is ready, spoon a little into one of the chilled dishes and place in the freezer for a few minutes. If it appears thickened, and a skin has formed that wrinkles when you drag your finger through it, it is ready. Otherwise simmer it for another 5 minutes and try again.

Put a few rosemary sprigs into each warm jar and fill them with the jelly. Cover with a clean kitchen towel and leave to cool for a couple of hours or until the jelly has begun to set, then press the herbs down to suspend them. Re-cover the jelly and leave to cool to room temperature, then seal and leave overnight. The jelly should keep well, stored in a cool environment, for several months.

*A jelly bag is a muslin sack sewn onto a wooden hoop. It can be hooked over a cabinet knob above a counter with the bowl beneath. In the absence of a hooped jelly bag, make your own: Open a wire hanger into a circle and attach a clean kitchen towel or old clean pillowcase over the rim to form a bag. Tie two long string handles opposite each other, to hang it up.

index